Praise for
Mad Money Journey – A Financial Adventure

"A wonderful engaging book about a wonderfully offbeat study of that little understood phenomenon – money."

—Ratan Tata

"Blew my mind. How could finance be so gripping? A ground-breaking combination of fiction and finance. Mehrab seems to have pulled off a near – impossible feat. This is a reflective novel written in an introspective manner – but this is also a deeply suspenseful work, the sense of anticipation heightened by Mehrab's wonderful use of restraint. When will this story be turned into a movie?"

—Cyrus Broacha

"Finance is turned to fiction by the imagination of Mehrab. And then he makes it a story, a fable, a page – turner, a suspenseful thrilling journey which when experienced will make you permanently change the way you look at life and money."

—Rakesh Jhunjhunwala

"An engaging story that draws you in and subtly teaches important financial lessons. A surprise package as I found myself as interested in the drama unfolding as in the tips on money management!"

—Tara Sharma

Mad

MONEY

JOURNEY

A Financial Adventure

Mad

MONEY

JOURNEY

A Financial Adventure

MEHRAB IRANI

JAICO PUBLISHING HOUSE

Ahmedabad Bangalore Bhopal Bhubaneswar Chennai
Delhi Hyderabad Kolkata Lucknow Mumbai

Published by Jaico Publishing House
A-2 Jash Chambers, 7-A Sir Phirozshah Mehta Road
Fort, Mumbai - 400 001
jaicopub@jaicobooks.com
www.jaicobooks.com

MAD MONEY JOURNEY
ISBN 978-81-8495-577-4

First Jaico Impression: 2014
Tenth Jaico Impression: 2015

Printed by
Repro India Limited
Plot No. 50/2, T.T.C. MIDC Industrial Area
Mahape, Navi Mumbai - 400 710

This book is dedicated to all those people whom I have met and will meet in this incredible life as the invisible hands of time carry me forward to unimaginable ascent.

This book is dedicated to all who have guided me on my path toward true freedom.

Contents

Acknowledgments

One realizes that being successful in life is greatly due to the people that one meets along the way. I've always felt that to take sole credit for one's achievements is an unappreciative way to lead one's life. My acknowledgements to all the various people who have come into my life and had some kind of impact on me. My deepest gratitude to all those people who have always been a constant support and encouragement. Above all, I acknowledge the irreplaceable help of my greatest critics: it was because of them that I was always pushed to revisit my limits, and the more I stretched my limits, the more they expanded. Without them, it would not have been possible for me to advance on my mission of gifting you financial freedom. I am deeply grateful to all those who have helped me in my attempts to free you from the shackles of monetary slavery. I also acknowledge the help of fellow seekers, those brave people who exercise the courage to leave the crowd and deal with money as it is to be dealt with.

My deepest appreciation to the entire team at Jaico for the support that they have given me and my book. I would like to specifically thank Laksmi and Usha, who have worked extensively on the editing of this book. Special thanks to Sandhya Iyer, Deputy Managing Editor at Jaico, for the invaluable editorial inputs. It would be wrong if I did not thank my publisher, Akash Shah, who understood my concept and idea from the very beginning. His innovative thoughts, timely advice and professional approach toward his duty made me a much better writer. I would also like to offer my sincere thanks to the sales, marketing and publicity department at Jaico, Vijay Thakur and his team, who left no stone unturned in creating a special brand for the book.

There are two people in this world who have never been appreciated enough – Mom and Dad. It is they who nurtured me and gave me an opportunity to enter this world and be of service to humanity. I am short of words to describe their contribution in my life. I shall just close my eyes, take a deep breath and say thank you to them.

My sincere thanks to my 8-year-old daughter, Simone Irani. It is she who reminds me daily of the need for financial education. She makes me realize the importance of fables and stories in the whole learning process. Every night, as I read out bedtime stories to her, I realize that we never really grow up; we just learn to act mature in public, but in our hearts, we are alike. Whether it's a child or an adult, the best way to learn is through a story and everybody can relate to a story about life and money. Each person should be able to identify with the characters emotionally and, simultaneously, imbibe the immense and valuable education on finance and money presented here. My daughter made me realize that I had to write a book combining my knowledge and understanding of money and life. In a gentle way, she taught me the best secret of my life.

Last but certainly not the least, I express my utmost acknowledgement to my better half, my companion, advisor, and savior – my wife, Shirin Irani. It is Shirin who made me realize that I can make a difference to this world. She taught me to teach others and made me realize that through my writing, I can indeed change lives for the betterment of humanity. It is my wife who made me successfully take the long journey from a *human being* and to *being human*.

Prologue

It is 6.30 pm. The sun is slowly melting into the horizon. The horned moon begins his laborious climb. I am lying on the hospital bed, waxing poetic while I breathe what might be my last few breaths.

Through weakened old eyes, I see my children, grandchildren and their children. My beautiful, faithful wife sits bone straight beside my bed, though I can tell her shoulders ache. I hear doctors and nurses hurrying around, buzzing, trying their best, the last medicine, the final injection, an ultimate attempt to save this sagging body. I hear a crowd of voices from the hospital corridor arguing with the doctors, enquiring, pleading and some even shouting at the doctor to save me. I feel a multitude gathered in the hospital compound, all waiting for me to recover, perhaps to appear at the window and wave a dramatically recovered hand at them.

But then, who am I? A rock star? A celebrity cricketer? A leader? No, I am just an ordinary man. But one who taught other men how to win over money in life.

Before all, I am John Pinto and this is my story. It is also the story of my incredible friend, Vijay Desai, who rescued me the first time I put myself in death's way. And it is a story woven from my journey to far-flung corners of the earth, where Vijay sent me to meet the most mysterious and extraordinary people. They generously showered me with their wealth of experience and knowledge, becoming my most invaluable teachers. Their wisdom showed me the path to free humanity from its financial problems. It is this story that I wish to share before I leave.

My eyes go to the TV screen in the corner of the room. The channel shows a suburban railway station. A train draws into the station and a mad frenzy ensues as hundreds of passengers rush in and out of it for what seems like an eternity – old, young, weak, strong, bold, beautiful, disabled and more. People run to and fro and around each other, pushing and shoving. There was some job or some task to attend to, and all were on a journey toward earning money or the hope of earning money.

They are all bound to routines and schedules; to the next local train in this case. Some invisible whip drives them on to work like slaves. But this is a free country. What makes me think they are slaves? Perhaps it is because I too was a part of this system once and can sympathize. I was once a slave to my orthodox way of life and money-wage slave of the employer, tax slave of the government and loan slave of the bank. I was a prisoner of money. But that was long ago. And before I run out of time, I want to free humanity from the shackles of financial slavery. I want to gift each one of them their birthright – financial freedom.

So without further ado, I will begin the story.

A Fortuitous Meeting

My eyes snapped open and as I surveyed the room, I realized with growing horror that I was lying on a hospital bed, hooked up to bottles of blood and glucose.

What had happened?

As the fog in my mind cleared, I visualized walking unsteadily through the fast-moving traffic of Marine Drive, Mumbai. Slowly, I recollected popping an overdose of sleeping pills and getting behind the wheel of my car. After driving for almost 30 minutes, I parked in front of one of the gymkhanas and started walking. When the pills started taking effect, I saw a water fountain on the other side of the road and made a dash for it, hoping to overcome my drowsiness with a splash of water. But I never made it and collapsed in the middle of the road.

A car came to a screeching halt within inches of me. A well-built man about my age, with the help of others, lifted me on to his car.

And that's when I passed out.

When I regained consciousness, I couldn't help but wonder why I had overdosed on those pills. I was a 45-year-old respected orthopedic surgeon, with a loving wife, Mary, a smart son, Allen, 20, studying to become a tax consultant, a beautiful daughter, Rose, just past her 18th birthday, and a doting mother.

Our house, on the 46th floor of one of Central Mumbai's iconic skyscrapers, looked out on this sprawling city, while my clinic was located in a posh neighborhood of South Mumbai. My chauffeur-driven Mercedes E series was just one symbol of my professional success as head of the orthopedic department of one of the city's most prestigious hospitals.

I was the envy of many for having both a great family and financial wealth.

But was I really wealthy?

Lying on that hospital bed, I began to mull over my investments. Most were in fully taxable fixed deposits, whose values were being constantly eroded by inflation. My meager allocations to equities were only in high-growth but risky, mid-cap stocks which were bleeding in the recent stock market collapse. Although I was earning handsomely, I did not know how to protect my money from financial predators who literally stole from my pocket at every stage, be it earning, saving, spending, leveraging, investing or insuring it. I was practically earning it for others – from my milkman and the government to the banker – but not for myself. I paid myself no portion of my own hard-earned money.

I was guilty of innumerable common financial mistakes, such as mental accounting, loss avoidance, decision paralysis and selective thinking among others, which led me to take all the wrong decisions. My heart sank at the thought of how I had taken negative leverages to buy my posh house and how I was reeling under the oppressive interest burden. I went for even more negative leverage to buy a capital asset, such as the car that I bought for my daughter's birthday.

I had over-invested in speculative, non-income yielding items such as gold. And I did not have adequate financial insurance for my assets, including my biggest one – my ability to earn. How could I forget the massive heart attack that almost paralyzed the right side of my body and put me out of work for nearly a year. Although I recovered, I had suffered both physically and emotionally because of the lack of proper financial insurance.

I now understood the reasons that had driven me, an obedient son, loving husband and caring father, to the brink of suicide.

As these thoughts played havoc on my mind, I saw my lovely wife and children entering the hospital room. Her tearful eyes and the look of hurt on my children's faces were more than I could bear. *Where did I go wrong in my love and duty toward you and the family?* Mary's quiet sobs screamed. *Why, dad, did you want to leave me just as I had dared to begin dreaming?* my son's accusing eyes said. *Did you celebrate my 18th birthday, only so you could leave me grieving for the rest of my life,* said my daughter's gaze, stabbing my heart. The worst was to see my old mother, hobbling in with her walking stick. What right did I have to take the life that was her gift to me?

As I struggled to answer their unspoken questions, I saw a tall, well-built gentleman striding confidently into the room. He had a different radiance: his eyes sparkling, skin glowing and hair shining. He seemed somewhat close to my age, but looked much younger, stronger and happier.

"How are you, John Pinto?" he asked. I suddenly recognized that voice. He was the one who lifted me on to his car before I blacked out. But, wait, there was something else that seemed familiar.

"So John, do you remember me? I'm the one who saved you and admitted you to this hospital," he said.

"Thank you," I muttered, self-consciously.

"Happy to know you recognize me," he said, a tad sarcastically.

My mother grinned on hearing this and I became more confused. He then asked if I remembered the young goalkeeper of my childhood days, the one who always had to be bailed out by the player in center-back position.

As I took a trip down memory lane, I suddenly remembered I was the goalkeeper who never really saved any goals.

"I was that goalkeeper," I said.

"Ah, so you remember the goalkeeper, but not the one who helped him save the goals?" he asked.

My mind started rewinding spontaneously as the glossy pictures of my childhood became clear in front of me. I now visibly remembered Vijay Desai – my friend and savior. How could I forget him? He used to mark me present when I could not attend classes; help me cut open a mango with his stone tools when I fancied one; cheerfully forgo his lunch money to buy me an ice cream; and help me copy his answers during exams.

On one occasion, when my father was not able to pay my school fees, it was Vijay who sold his cycle to make the payment. He was the friend who walked into my life when the others had walked out.

We stayed opposite one another in what is known as a *chawl* – a series of small rooms with shared toilet facilities. Being a Catholic, I lived in a building primarily occupied by Catholics, while Vijay lived in a Hindu dominated one. Our buildings were separated by a narrow lane, at the end of which stood a government school where the poorer children studied. Vijay and I attended a school that was just a 5-minute walk from our homes and was the choice of middle-class families like ours. We spent many evenings playing cricket and football in those narrow lanes. A sidewall served as the stumps for cricket, while a building gate would double as the goalpost for a game of football. Our audience was the many vegetable and fruit vendors whose homes lined the lanes.

My father worked for a government-owned bank, while Vijay's father was employed by a government company. In short, we both belonged to the typical, vast, middle-class population of so-called growing India. Being government servants, our fathers stressed the importance of a good education to secure a good job, preferably with the government. I took their lessons to heart, studying hard, earning good grades and qualifying for medical school. However, Vijay never agreed with either his father or mine. From an early age, he thought differently about money. He never agreed to become a slave to money by working for it. Even when we were in high school, he would say that the only thing available in abundance in this world is money. When we lost a football, all of us would fret over how we would come up with the money for a new one, except for Vijay. He would say we should be more worried about the limited availability of the materials, like rubber and leather, that went into the making of a football. He would claim that money was always available at the free will of governments, who could print as much currency as their printing machines could churn out. Although both of us grew up believing in the value of education, we had radically different views of what education was all about. While I subscribed to the traditional idea of going to school, studying hard and earning a professional degree, Vijay saw education as something that would expand one's knowledge and understanding, not just something that would help one score well in exams.

To him, education was making mistakes and learning from them, not avoiding failure for fear of being called stupid by teachers, parents or other students. To him, education was a journey beginning from the cradle and ending with the grave, not with the earning of a degree. To him, education was the freedom to do whatever you wanted in life, rather than becoming a slave to your profession. It was financial independence, where your money works for you, instead of you working for money.

From a very young age, Vijay showed that he had a mind of his own. He refused to be a slave to old ideas and unsurprisingly, was not very well-liked by the principal, teachers, other students, or even his own parents. But this never daunted him. He hated being compared with others, saying every person is unique and comparing two people was an insult to both of them.

Vijay failed in his tenth standard final exams. His parents disowned him, ridiculing and humiliating him for his failure. He decided to pack his bags and head out into the real world, convinced his ideas would find fertile ground outside the confines of his parental home. He firmly believed that with patience, perseverance, hard work, a true mentor, good friends and the right inspiration, backed by the power of learning from life, he would achieve great success.

When he stopped by to bid me farewell I was standing tall with my high school certificate. I had not only topped in my school but also in my city. I was full of dreams of becoming the best medical surgeon, not only in India but also the whole world.

He said, "John, I have left my parents' home and am moving into the real world, where a wealth of opportunities await me. I want to be genuinely true to myself even when everyone around me wants to be someone else. True success is about believing in ourselves when no one else does. I don't know where I will go, with whom I will live, or even what I will do, but I know that I will get real education that will teach me to become financially independent. I don't know if I'll see you again, but if life so desires, we will surely meet one day." Given his position then, anyone would have thought these were the arrogant thoughts of a weak teenager going out into the big, bad world for the first time. But actually, it was coming from a very confident, young lad with a keen sense of money that belied his age. He had incredible courage of conviction and a strong belief in God. However, at that point of time, it appeared to me as though he were embarking on a suicidal mission. I had no idea what to say to him then.

But 30 years on, it was me, the qualified doctor with a caring mother, a beautiful wife and two loving children, who had tried to commit suicide. And it was Vijay Desai, my childhood friend, who had actually saved me. How did that young lad who had failed his high school exams and left the security of his parents' home, become this symbol of success and achievement? The Vijay Group of Industries had businesses in many fields, including iron and steel, oil and petrochemicals, textiles, automobiles, entertainment, telecom and real estate. He had spread his wings not only in India, but also abroad. He was a business tycoon, who attracted governments, ministers, politicians, film stars, sports personalities and inspirational gurus. And despite being 45, young girls still pined for him, for his charismatic looks and visionary acts.

He was the same person who had once been ridiculed by his parents, teachers and fellow students, including myself. He had simply brushed it off saying the more you worry about being applauded by others and making money, the less you focus on doing the work that will actually generate applause and money.

A confident voice interrupted my thoughts.

"So, my friend, how have you been?"

There was Vijay standing before me, the high school dropout looking every inch the successful business tycoon in his Armani suit and blue-colored tie. A red handkerchief hung from his pocket and his graying hair was combed to perfection. At 15, he was a failure, whom no one wanted to emulate. While at 45, he was a visionary businessman, industrialist and philanthropist, even a glimpse of him was like a dream come true. Conversely, at the age of 15, I was a brilliant student, having topped both my high school and the entire city. While at the age of 45, I was a middle-class doctor and still broke. Instead of giving life to others, I had become the enemy of his own life. As Vijay put his hand on mine and looked at me with the same friendly gaze reminiscent of my childhood, I struggled to hold back my tears and answered bravely, "getting along."

"John, you are a successful doctor with a loving family. What prompted you to take such a drastic step?" he asked.

"I'm having problems, financial problems, and don't know whom to turn to."

"Don't worry. Your school friend is back to once again save your goal. But my ideas are still as unorthodox as they were in school. I don't know if you will appreciate them."

"You've proved us all wrong. You failed the school exams, but topped life's exams, whereas I topped the school exams only to fail miserably in life."

Looking at me with some concern, I could see he held a unique sense of faith in me. He simply smiled and wished me goodbye, saying he had to attend an important meeting, but promised to be back soon.

I was discharged from the hospital a couple of days later. The doctor waved me away, cheerfully saying, "you are perfectly fine, now. Go on and cure your patients."

I had told my family not to pick me up. As I made my way slowly through the hospital corridors, watching the patients and their anxious relatives, I felt weighed down in mind, body and soul. What was I returning to? Where was my life headed? I may have been a very successful doctor, but I was very unsuccessful in financial matters. I could take care of my patients, but not my own money.

The sun hurt my eyes as I stood outside pondering over these questions. It was as though I had gotten used to the darkness engulfing my life. Just then, a smartly dressed man appeared in front of me and said politely, "sir, kindly come this way. The car is parked over there." He pointed to a red Jaguar, as he held out the card of the person who had sent him.

It read: *Vijay Desai, Chairman, Vijay Group of Industries.*

My friend had kept his promise.

I marveled at the beauty of the car's exterior and interior as I slowly climbed into it. The driver started the engine as I was wearing my seatbelt and the car took off like a ride in heaven. I had never been in a chauffeur-driven luxury car before.

On reaching Vijay's spanking new 25-floor office, I was escorted by a charming, young lady called Reena, who introduced herself as one of Vijay's personal assistants. She led me past a shining lobby full of sparkling glass to his personal luxurious rooftop office .

Settling into one of the cushioned seats of a beautifully furnished conference room, I caught sight of my friend's face staring at me from the cover of one of the nation's top business magazines. Vijay had been named, 'Businessman of the Year'!

I wondered if I could still call myself the friend of such a great personality. He was miles ahead of me in terms of money and wealth, as well as financial knowledge and wisdom.

While I digested these thoughts and feelings, Reena signaled me to follow her into Vijay's personal chamber. A marble-paneled corridor opened into a large room with floor-to-ceiling windows that offered a sweeping view of the harborfront skyline. My friend greeted me courteously, asking if my journey from the hospital had been comfortable.

I seated myself across him at a teakwood table. After quickly scanning his laptop, he finally turned to me.

"So, my friend, you are a qualified, respected doctor, and yet, you are so broke that you want to quit life altogether? Is this where your education has taken you after topping the school exams that I had failed? Back then, you never understood me or my ideas on money and life. You would ridicule me when I disagreed with your traditional dead ideas about education and wealth. Now, look who's in trouble," he said without mincing his words.

As the tears started rolling down my face, Vijay softened.

"I didn't mean to insult you. I respect you. You are a very accomplished doctor. But being a successful doctor doesn't automatically make you a successful money person. Just as the right medicine is required to cure a disease, you should also know the right financial commandments to solve various financial issues."

I stared at him in amazement, "the right financial commandments? What are those, Vijay?"

He then went on to explain the ten financial commandments that govern how a person deals with money while earning, protecting, budgeting, saving, spending, leveraging, investing and insuring it.

"Each commandment explains how to deal with money at every stage of life. It also explains the rules of money."

"Rules of money?" I asked incredulously.

"Yes," Vijay said, "everything in this world has rules. Schools, offices, hospitals, courts and governments, all have rules, so why not money as well, when it's one the most important things on earth?"

Seeing my confusion, he explained further, "money is subject to different rules. For example, money can't be the solution to your problems. You have to be the master of your own money. You don't have to run after money when it's available in abundance."

Astonished, I repeated, "money is available in abundance, but money can't be the solution."

"That's right," Vijay said confidently.

"Money can't be the solution, if you think money is your problem."

"Have you ever heard of the problem itself being the solution?"

I said that while I understood that a problem cannot also be its own solution, how could money be available in abundance when so many people were poor?

"So many people are poor because they don't understand, accept and apply the financial commandments. As to the abundance of money, remember that it is available at the free will of the government as it can print money as fast as its printers work."

I was gradually beginning to get the drift of what he was saying.

"But what do you mean when you say don't run after money? In reality, we have to work hard for money and many times run after it."

He laughed and said, "that is another folly of the poor and the middle-class. They always run after money and are never able to catch it, because if you run after it, it will only run away from you faster. However, if you learn how to make money work for you, it will become your slave and run after you wherever you go. Have you ever heard the proverb that says never run after a train, bus or woman – 'one goes, another one comes along'?"

I jumped out of my chair in agreement. It was perhaps the first thing that I had completely understood since we met.

"I will add money to that list," he said more seriously.

"As long as you're working for your money, you'll be living for earned income. This is the income you work the hardest for, pay the highest in taxes, keep a minimum to save, meanwhile it gets eaten away by the monster of inflation. You are ignorant to spending it intelligently, to investing it to increase your wealth, to multiplying it through positive leverage and to insuring yourself and your wealth."

The financial jargon was confusing and annoyed me a little. "Vijay, if I were only to use medical jargon, would you understand anything? Then how do you expect a doctor without any financial background to understand this?"

He took a deep breath as the conversation was taking a rather serious turn. He said, "you are a doctor, but who am I – a high school dropout. Which financial degree allowed me to learn all this? I have learned all this from life and money. Would you prefer increasing your financial knowledge and achieving financial independence, or ignoring the financial commandments and becoming a slave to money for life?" I answered quickly and without hesitation, "of course, I would like to achieve financial independence."

"That's it, my friend!" Vijay smiled.

Further expanding on his ideas, he continued, "if you want financial independence, you must first become acquainted with the financial commandments. I want you to know that asset allocation is of primary importance, as 90% of portfolio variability is due to asset allocation, while only 10% of the variability in portfolio performance is due to market timing and stock selection.

I want you to protect your money from the legal financial predators. You need to appreciate the importance of budgeting and paying yourself before paying others. You also have to be wary of falling prey to common financial mistakes. Be aware of the principles governing investment in equities and other asset classes. Learn how to unleash the ultimate power of positive leverage. You should also know that your house is a bad capital asset, not an investment asset and why you should own a house only for self-occupation.

Grasp why you should invest to generate running income and not asset income and, therefore, why you must not over-invest in speculative items, like gold. Then I would urge you to realize the value of taking financial insurance, which will protect you against everything that could come between you and your money."

I was completely stunned by all this and downed the glass of water sitting on the table in one quick gulp.

"Don't worry, my friend," said Vijay amused, "this was just the introduction to the financial commandments. They will change your perspective on how you view money. They will teach you that both a lack of money and an excess of it can be a problem if not backed by financial knowledge on in managing it. They don't teach you how to get rich quickly, but how to systematically plan its protection, preservation and wealth development. So, you don't just become comfortably rich enough to contribute to charity, you also remain wealthy throughout your life. The commandments talk about money, its intricacies and its functioning in a manner never done before. They are as useful to a seasoned professional investor as to a naïve lay investor. They're also useful to today's youth who might earn a lot, but don't know how to protect their money from financial predators. They pay everybody without budgeting for themselves. Without proper investments and positive leverage, their money becomes prey to the monsters of inflation, taxation and market volatility."

He told me he, too, lived by these commandments and his sprawling business empire was a by-product of their wisdom.

"But first, let me clear some common misconceptions about money. Remember how I said you don't have to be a slave to money? By working for money, you get earned income. However, when your money works for you in the form of a bank deposit, earning interest, or equity stock earning dividend, or rental real estate earning rent, the money earns you a guaranteed or passive income. And when you, at a future date, sell and realize a profit from an investment asset which has appreciated in value during your holding period, it becomes portfolio income. Therefore, you can sit and relax, because you have reached financial nirvana."

"That's fantastic!" I said enthusiastically, but Vijay had only touched the tip of the iceberg.

"Money has two peculiar problems," he observed with a cunning smile. "Problem of excess money and problem of scarcity of money." Before I could say anything, he added, "if you have more money than you can possibly spend in your lifetime, but are still crazy for money, then obviously you are a very unhappy person with only money for companionship. However, there are others who have money, but don't possess the knowledge to manage it, which can amount to a very dangerous situation. These are the people who have received money through inheritance, lottery or gambling, or are some sort of celebrity. They acquire surplus money quickly without gaining any knowledge about money. And, finally, what is money? It is nothing but paper currency, and if you don't know how to bear the current of it, then either it will burn you or it will burn itself. Just as electricity keeps flowing from one circuit to another, similarly money will keep flowing from one person to another, unless you know how to use its potential to light up your house."

Pretty interesting observation. I had to admit I had never thought about money this way and I surely wanted to now learn more about its peculiarities.

As I was thinking things through, a uniformed boy entered the chamber along with a helper carrying some delicious food and drinks. I smelled my favorite chicken kebabs − tikka, *reshmi* and *seekh* − along with delicious mutton biryani. He had also ordered my favorite wine. It was commendable that despite being so rich and famous, my friend still remembered what my favorite dishes were. I felt fortunate to be sitting in front of such a great personality, dining with him in his office and learning about money. "Is the menu right?" he enquired, "or did I forget something?"

I replied feeling slightly ashamed, "no buddy, its perfect. Thanks."

"Look here," he said firmly, "you may bad-mouth me, but don't ever say thanks or sorry." I nodded in assent.

As I mulled over these ideas through the meal, he started on my problem, the scarcity of money. "Your problem is not having less money, but the belief that you have less money and that it will never be enough. What is money in today's modern world?

Is it some precious metal like gold, whose supply is limited; or real estate, which can't be expanded beyond this world; or a perishable item like fruits and vegetables, which can't be stored beyond a few hours or days? No. Money is neither perishable, nor is its supply limited. Money is simply an idea, a thought whose time has come. If you have an idea, no one can stop you from becoming rich. There are many rich people out there waiting to invest in some kind of profitable venture. Positive leverage is easily available in today's modern banking system. The point I want to make here is that the problem is not money, but the lack of knowledge about it. Remember that in any field, whether business, sports or movies, it's easy to reach the number one position, but very difficult to retain that position. When you're successful, it's very easy to stop doing the very things that made you successful in the first place. Financial knowledge the working of money are the answers to not only becoming rich, but staying wealthy for generations to come."

I was so overwhelmed by this spectacular revelation, that I had forgotten about the kebabs that were getting cold due to the air-conditioning. Vijay soon reminded me, but instead of enjoying the taste of my favorite food, my mind was now trying to recollect, assimilate and digest what I had just heard.

We topped off our meal with a chocolate-laced cappuccino, just the way Vijay remembered I always liked it. He said, "I'm going to send you on a month-long vacation around the world. You will visit certain extraordinary individuals in their respective town, house or workplace. They are the living embodiments of the financial commandments. They haven't only understood and accepted them, but have also applied them in their day-to-day lives. You'll live with each one of them for a few days, so as to actually see and feel how it is to live by the commandments. When your stay is over, each one of them will hand you a letter carrying the wisdom of a particular commandment. The wisdom will introduce you to a new world of possibilities. They will teach you not only about money, but also certain divine principles of life. Your mind, body and soul will be enriched - you'll be a new man, my friend, lifted from the base of the ordinary into the higher realms of the extraordinary."

He told me that my search for these wisdoms would commence from the next day. He had already informed my family about the *mad money journey* that I was about to undertake and was kind enough to arrange for my luggage.

"I really thank you for all this," I said. "Will you give me my schedule now?" To which he smiled and said, "that's a good question, but I can't give you your schedule at this point of time. The wisdom from the financial commandments has to be accepted, understood, appreciated, lived and remembered throughout. So, the lessons you learn on your journey can't be scheduled. What I can tell you is that this marvelous journey of wisdom begins from Bangkok, Thailand. The lady you meet there will help you with your finances. Once you are done, she will give you the information to your next destination. This is how your schedule will establish itself."

Warming to this idea, I said, "then what is the first nugget of wisdom you have to offer, since you are the first person I have met?"

In a steely tone, Vijay told me that it was lying on the backseat of the car that would take me home.

"Go, read, learn, understand, appreciate and accept it. Lots of it will be coming your way over the next few weeks. And yes, do enjoy your world trip. But, before you go, I want you to promise me something." "What's that?" I asked suspiciously.

"Don't worry, I'm not asking for anything material," he replied, taking a long breath.

"I want you to gain the courage necessary to pass on the gift of the financial commandments and the wisdom thereof to as many people as you can. That's all, my friend."

It was a fair request and I agreed to it. Then I thanked him, eager to read the first letter of financial wisdom. I quickly walked through the aisle passing through the marvelous interiors of his office into the glass lobby to the main door. I jumped into the car waiting outside. I had forgotten to wear the seat belt in my excitement to find the letter, but the driver promptly reminded me. Then I found a small memento, containing the picture of a school embossed on it. Tied to it with a red ribbon was an envelope. I immediately untied the ribbon and removed the letter.

Rules of Money and Life

Just as a school runs on discipline and rules, money, too, is subject to its own peculiar rules.

Excess money can be as much of a problem as its scarcity. True financial independence comes not with money, but with knowledge of the financial commandments and the wisdom emanating from them. The only thing available in abundance in this world is money. Never work for money, but make your money work for you (guaranteed, passive and portfolio income). Learn the right way to deal with money at every stage, whether earning, protecting, budgeting, saving, spending, leveraging, investing or insuring it, for sustainable, long-term wealth creation. Don't look for ways to get rich quickly, instead work on a systematic plan to protect, preserve and grow your wealth. Money cannot be dealt with in isolation, but must be viewed in totality with other aspects of life. Only if you are true to yourself and are able to respect and protect your family, will you be able to protect and grow your money. To double your net worth, first double your self-worth. Have the guts to see opportunities where others view them as setbacks. All problems, in effect, are opportunities in disguise. The more you worry about being applauded by others and making money, the less you will focus on doing the work that will actually generate applause and money. All great thinkers are initially condemned and eventually respected. With the increase in knowledge of money and life, don't feel great but be grateful that God has selected you as his instrument to pass on this knowledge. This way, you are certain to experience fortune well beyond your wildest imagination.

Common Mistakes

I was in high spirits throughout the flight to Bangkok. It was my first trip to Southeast Asia. I wondered about the lady I was going to meet. Would she be one of Thailand's prominent businesswomen? Someone equal to Vijay in fame and riches? Perhaps a teacher? My thoughts were interrupted by a tall, beautiful flight attendant carrying a tray.

"Your meal, sir," she said in a sweet voice. I dug into the delicious Thai food with gusto. When my meal was over, my mind went back to everything that Vijay had said – the rules of money and life, problem of excess and scarcity of money, pitfalls of getting rich quickly, the abundance of money, intricacies and functioning of money and that knowledge of all this could lead to a fortune beyond one's wildest imagination. I soon fell into deep sleep.

I woke up suddenly to the captain's voice urging passengers to wear their seat belts. As I looked out of the window, the flight began its descent to the first rays of the morning sun.

I made my way to the exit with my luggage and was greeted by a young man of dark complexion with chinky eyes, long hair and a birth mark on his face.

"I am Clive Attapakee, your escort," he said. He was a man of few words and we rode to our destination in silence. As we snaked our way through the bustling city, I marveled at the glass-paneled skyscrapers framed by hills on the far horizon.

But slowly this scene began to change. Tree-lined avenues gave way to narrow streets; modern brick buildings were replaced by small wooden houses with curling roofs and ornate trims. I saw groups of women huddled on street corners, waiting, watching and beckoning with their magnetic eyes. I also saw many storefront signboards that read 'massage parlors', 'Thai massage' and 'soapy massage' among others. I wondered where we were headed, when Clive said, "we are almost there," pointing to a narrow lane to his right. The car turned into it and slowed to a halt in front of a small building.

As I stepped out, I saw several scantily dressed girls, barely adults, eyeing me curiously. Clive shouted at them in their native tongue and they quickly dispersed. He then led me through a narrow staircase to an apartment on the first floor. The room I entered was small, its floor covered in tiny white tiles, and its wooden walls lined with hand-held shower faucets. In front of each faucet stood a small wooden stool and a small bucket. In the farthest corner of the room was a table with some chairs placed casually around it. The room was warm and humid.

A middle-aged woman in a loose top, short skirt, high-heeled shoes and loud jewelry greeted me. "*Sawatdee Ka* (good morning), I am Duan Aimond, Vijay's friend. How was your journey?" she enquired.

"Fine, Duan," I said as I sat on a chair and took in my surroundings.

"So what do you do over here," I asked Duan, curious about all the girls I had seen on my way here. Her answer confirmed my initial suspicions.

"They are massage girls; in other words, prostitutes. I rehabilitate them, provide them food and shelter and try to find them some kind of job. And if they have families, I try to reunite them."

"Have you been doing this for a long time?" I asked.

"I used to be like them." Ignoring my astonishment, she added, "in fact, I used to be a porn star."

I was stunned. Vijay had sent me across an ocean to learn about financial wisdom from a former porn star?

Anger and indignation reared their ugly heads. Before I could say anything, a girl entered the room carrying food and a menu card that read: *tom kha kai* (coconut milk soup), *yum talay* (seafood salad), Chiang Mia's *khao soi* noodles, *panang* curry and ice cream. The aroma of these Thai delicacies was so tempting that for a brief moment I forgot Duan's shocking revelation. I was only reminded of it when I looked up to catch Duan giving me a cold look.

"You probably know only as much about massage girls, prostitutes and porn stars as you know about money," she said.

"What a strange comparison," I retorted.

"Let me show you how they are connected. Just as you have never succeeded in your job, I, a prostitute, have never thrived in my profession, simply because neither of us has loved our jobs."

"Don't you love your job – sex?" I asked curiously.

"I do like sex, but not as a job; not having sex with a stranger or in front of a camera, because that sex is not for my pleasure, but for the entertainment of a client."

It suddenly made sense to me. This was a whole new perspective on sex, prostitution and porn. I felt I had to know how she ended up in this profession.

"I am the oldest of five in a farming family of Phetchabun," she said. "My father was poor, not because his land was barren or because there were no buyers for his produce, but because of his bad habit of throwing good money after bad. For example, even when he had a bad crop and it was best to let go, he would try his utmost to save it. In the end, he would lose all our money over it."

I knew that I, too, was guilty of basing many financial decisions on past actions, even when it was clear they had been the wrong ones. I remembered especially how I persisted with a bad insurance policy and continued to pay premiums just to protect premiums I had paid in the past. This pattern of behavior is referred to as *sunk cost fallacy*.

Duan then went on to explain how her parents held on to losing assets just to avoid booking the loss. When one of their cows became diseased, they could have given up her care to an NGO, knowing they did not have the money to cure the animal. When they didn't do this, the cow eventually died. "We lost the cow and the cow lost its life." In other words, they had succumbed to *loss avoidance*.

My mind went back to all those times I had resisted selling my loss-making investments, like in the case of the sick cow, just to avoid the psychological pain of booking the loss, even as I sold my good, profitable investments, the holy cows, which were giving me income in the form of dividends.

"Many times, when the fruits or vegetables my father grew became rotten, he would still keep them in the expectation that someone would pay him a good price for them. He would pay the warehouse rent, block his capital, pay interest on the holding cost and waste his precious time trying to market them. That would not only lose him money on the perishables, but also not allow him to capitalize on the growth opportunity ahead."

I thought of all those times I had been swayed by the idea of gaining a certain amount of money, when the loss accruing from the same decision was actually more. I was victim to what behavioral theorists call *prospect theory*.

Duan also complained bitterly about how her father dealt with the land he inherited from an aunt who had no heirs. He would, Duan said, take all kinds of risks with it, like growing certain banned items, carrying out illegal activities, borrowing by mortgaging it, gambling against its value, as he had mentally accounted for it as something free. Eventually, he lost this free wealth.

I thought, shamefaced, of how I was guilty of the same mental accounting when it came to my performance awards. Despite winning it seven of the ten times it was awarded, I had frittered it all away. I felt really stupid. I had, on numerous occasions spent any windfall gain, including from lottery tickets which were small in value, because I never won big and other such sums of money.

Duan's life story was surely becoming a lesson in financial management and there was more to come.

"People are often paralyzed into inaction," she said. "Many a time they are unable to take a decision and by not being proactive, they actually take a decision in favor of maintaining the status quo.

When my younger brother wanted to go to college, my parents could not make up their minds as to whether he should go or join the family business instead. Thanks to their dithering, my brother remained in the business, underemployed."

The same *decision paralysis* had stopped me from allowing my wife to take her final year law exam and join the legal profession. I had forced her to become a housewife, sacrificing not only her career, but also her self-worth.

My new friend then went on to narrate how her parents would always look for answers that confirmed their existing beliefs, whether dealing with their business, money or the lives of their children. For example, they were convinced that a man with family wealth, land and business would make a great husband for their daughter. They deliberately chose to ignore his education and personality.

"My marriage was a disaster and that's one of the main reasons I ended up on the streets," she said visibly pained.

I wondered how many times had I, too, been guilty of similar thought patterns. I had always surrounded myself with people who said what I wanted to hear, and chose to ignore honest advice. I never took brokers and advisors seriously, and my stock and mutual funds portfolio were evidence of my *confirmation bias* and *selective thinking*.

I was to learn that these were not my only follies. Duan described how her parents believed that what they had was inherently superior to what others had, be it their agricultural produce, their livestock or their children.

"My father thought his fruit was better than that of his neighbor's; my mother was convinced her cow produced better milk than the neighbor's cow; and both were sure their son was the cleverest and their daughters the most beautiful."

"But they were right. Their daughter Duan is indeed very beautiful," I said.

"Have you ever experienced this in your own life?" Duan asked.

Of course, I said, and told her how I had held on to the sale price of my house, even when similar houses in the

vicinity were being sold at 10% lower than my asking price.
I held on to it till prices collapsed by another 15%, when I
was forced to foreclose it. This *endowment effect* has a good
number of people in its clutches.

"Then there are people who buy things they don't need,"
Duan continued. "As the great Warren Buffett once put it, 'if
you buy the things you don't require, then very soon you will
have to sell the things that you require'."

Such *buyer's remorse*, I knew, was fairly commonplace.
I marveled at how clever and well-read a porn star and a
prostitute she was, and here I was, a doctor, with literally
no knowledge about money and finance. My heart sank at
the thought of calling her a porn star and a prostitute. I
had developed great respect for her and imagined her as a
revolutionary savior of women and even men like myself. I
couldn't wait to hear more.

"You know, John, the things that give us happiness in
this world are those that come free, such as the splendor of a
glorious sunrise, the sweetness of birds chirping in the woods,
the magic of the moment when your child first calls you
dad or the warmth of your partner when she says she loves
you. These small but meaningful joys are always around us,
waiting to be explored and enjoyed, but we fail to recognize
them in our race for the bigger things in life. The same
goes for money. In our search for greater gains, we forget
the small, but important profits, which when compounded
over time, turn into something big. For example, small but
early and regular contributions to one's retirement fund will
make the kitty bigger, rather than late, sporadic and irregular
contributions to the wrong asset class."

I immediately thought of my own retirement fund, which
comprised mostly of fixed income instruments that were
slowly being eroded by the twin monsters of *tax* and *inflation*.

"Tell me, doctor, do you attend to your investments with the same alacrity as you do your patients needing emergency treatment? Do you do more research while buying socks or stocks?"

I was loath to admit that most of my investments were done casually based on market tips and the market sentiment.

Sensing my discomfort, she said, "the problem, John, is being overconfident, a common mistake people make while dealing with money or life. It is often the cause for much unhappiness. I lost my mother because of my father's overconfidence.

My mother had breast cancer, but my father thought it was just a fever and delayed the treatment. By the time he realized his mistake, it was too late," Duan said with tears in her eyes. I offered her my handkerchief in silent sympathy.

Later that evening after a rest, a luxurious bath with aromatic herbs and flowers and then authentic Thai ice tea, I joined Duan to trawl the streets of the city's red light districts. Teenagers waited at street corners for their customers, while I waited to continue my lessons on life and money. A boy, about 12, came up to Duan and offered her flowers. She turned to me and said, "I once rescued this boy from gay child prostitution. He comes from a wealthy family, but his father invested heavily in assets he knew nothing about. He then tried to hold on to those investments by pouring more and more money into them, spending recklessly with his credit card till he lost everything. The result? His wife left him for another rich man and this induced him to take his own life. The father's actions left this little boy an orphan."

I noticed numerous bar dancers moving around in rush hour, the same way office goers run in the morning toward their offices. "See these young girls," Duan said pointing to some prostitutes as we made our way through the narrow lanes crowded with tourists and pimps.

"They don't know their true worth and often undersell themselves. They believe they're not as beautiful as the next girl and so, are cutting their prices to unviable levels. Lack of confidence is a prime enemy of life and money. Many of us lose out on good investment opportunities, because of low confidence in our own abilities," she said.

So true! I knew gold was set to enter a great bullish phase for the next decade, but did precious little to change my portfolio, because of an innate lack of confidence in my own predictions. Gold did appreciate more than six times or by 500%, but I did not take advantage of it. *Lack of confidence* was affecting the wealth of as many prostitutes as investors around the world.

As we walked further, I noticed a young girl in a cab with four men. It looked like a group sex session was being negotiated.

"What you are witnessing is a classic example of *money illusion*," Duan said. "She is being exploited not only physically, but also monetarily."

Seeing me puzzled, she went on, "suppose her fee is US$25 per person, she should be paid US$100 for four men, but actually she will accept less, say US$75. She will think it is better than getting US$25. It is just like an employee with a 10% salary increment when the inflation is 12%, feeling he is better off than another employee getting a 5% increment when the inflation is 3%."

I marveled at Duan's finance savvy language. I also realized how foolish I was to invest in fixed deposits that yielded negative real interest rates after tax instead of in stocks yielding long-term, tax-free gains.

"I hope you are not offended by these comparisons with prostitutes," she asked.

"No, not at all," I responded, knowing they were selling their bodies simply to feed their families, while I had attempted to take my life and deprive my family of its bread winner.

We soon came upon what seemed like a dirt road. As I walked through the narrow lanes with buildings so decrepit that they looked like stone outcrops, I tried to picture how such a large number of girls survived in such tiny structures. Duan then pointed to a man and said, "look there, John. He's a pimp. Many girls have such agents who they believe will get them a better price than if they negotiate on their own. They also believe these men will protect them from the police and rogue clients. In return, they part with a substantial chunk of their earnings.

These agents are like your typical investment advisors. They provide you with options, but you believe they will also protect your investments against market volatility."

Whatever she said was indeed true. I remembered how many times I had been fooled by these so called investment advisors, who had just robbed me of my hard-earned money. I used to actually pay them fees for losing money!

As I went into self-realization mode, she poured out her knowledge to me, "I would like to quote Dr. William Bernstein, who once observed that, 'there are two kinds of investors, be they large or small – those who don't know where the market is headed, and those who don't know that they don't know where the market is headed. Then again, there is a third type of investor – the investment professional, who indeed knows that he or she doesn't know, but whose livelihood depends upon appearing to know where the market is headed'."

I was only now beginning to comprehend its true meaning. Suddenly, a long queue outside an ATM caught my eye. Noticing my curiosity, Duan said, "most of the patrons of this branch are the prostitutes. While men rob these girls of their dignity, the bank robs them of their money."

"Aren't banks supposed to protect our money?" I sputtered.

"Bankers are not there to make you money, but to make money for themselves. They don't even have to come and rob you. You willingly hand them your hard-earned savings!"

She went on to explain that bankers encouraged savings even as inflation eroded our purchasing power. Also, at the time of lending, they charge exorbitant interest rates through personal loans and credit cards, while encouraging people to buy liabilities like consumer durables and cars. Then, while dishing out investment advice, they charge high fees for substandard services.

This was hard-hitting stuff, a revelation, a transformation of thought, I had to admit. I had never thought of a bank as a robber of money and 'savings not being investments'. Most of my investments were bank deposits that earned a low rate of interest, which was fully taxable, even as inflation ate into the rest. My *after-tax* money was growing at a snail's pace, while my *purchasing power* was eroding at a cheetah's pace.

We then visited some famous Buddha temples in Bangkok – The Golden Buddha, The Reclining Buddha and The Principal Buddha. There in front of the Golden Buddha, Duan suddenly asked me slyly if I would like to indulge in a night of pleasure at one of the brothels. Offended, I replied that I was a committed family man.

"I was just testing you," she said. "If you don't have moral values, if you don't respect women, if you don't love your family and if you are not a good person, you can never be a good investor. You can never be a truly rich and wealthy person."

Duan continued with apparent disappointment, "you know, John, Siddhartha Gautama left his heavenly palace and all its worldly riches and pleasures to live the life of a monk and became the renowned 'Buddha'. But it's such a pity that after he left his body, people are making statutes of him in gold and other precious materials, the very same materials, which He left when alive to attain nirvana.

The real joy in life is not in collecting but in giving. And John, when you accumulate wealth after you learn the financial wisdoms, remember that you are owning all the wealth as a trustee of the people and do give it back to society." My head bowed in respect for this incredible woman.

Back in her house, I had to ask Duan how a person like her had ended up working in porn films. She promised to tell me the whole story the next day. We had another treat of sumptuous Thai delicacies after which I fell into deep slumber.

I woke up to the sound of some really soul-stirring music. Duan's house was bursting with activity; the sweepers were cleaning, cooks were preparing food and the gardener was watering the plants. Everybody was performing their duties in perfect harmony. But where was Duan? And where was this music coming from? On asking one of her servants, I came to know that Duan was fond of singing and was practicing on the roof of the building. I immediately got up to ascend to the roof, maneuvering my way up the narrow staircase. As I reached the rooftop, I saw Duan sitting opposite an old gentleman, who I presumed was her music guru. I sat quietly and watched her rehearse. I must admit her voice was as sweet as her face and her tone as deep as her heart. Her knowledge of music was probably as strong as her understanding of money.

After a few minutes, the maid brought in tea along with a traditional Thai breakfast, *johk*, a thick rice soup with pork balls, some liver and kidney along with partially cooked egg, sprinkled with shredded ginger. As I enjoyed the delicacy, Duan told me that she had always been passionate about music. "Whether it is music, life or money, you ought to love and respect it. Unless you do this how are you going to take care of it?" she asked.

How right she was. I had never respected money or my life. And so, I lost my money and was on the verge of losing my life.

The more I listened to Duan, the more keen I was to know her incredible journey from a prostitute and a porn star to a life saver: the turnaround from selling her body to earning money to making her money earn for her. My chance came that very afternoon.

"As I had mentioned earlier, I was the eldest of five children of a farmer in Phetchabun. I had three younger sisters and one brother. My father was poor simply because of his lack of financial knowledge. When I was 16, I fell in love with a classmate. He was a clever, hard-working student, who wanted to become a lawyer. But my father was opposed to the relationship, because he didn't have the vision that boy had. He wanted me to marry the spoiled brat of a rich landlord and forcibly married me to him. I was never happy with him, because of his horrid habits of drinking, smoking, gambling and going out with other girls and prostitutes. My husband had no respect, either for me or for the money that came to him from his father without his ever having to earn it! I gave birth to a daughter and when she was a year old, my husband threw us out."

She revealed softly with puffy eyes that she could not go back to her father's house, since he was struggling to make ends meet.

"I decided to pack my bags and head to Bangkok where a friend was working. She used to send home huge sums of money every month and I thought I would be able to do so, too. I left my baby in Phetchabun with my mother and took off, little realizing that I was about to enter hell. When my friend took me to the bar in Nana Plaza the first time, I received a rude shock."

She said she initially just served drinks, but then she realized that the pole dancers earned much more and decided to join them.

But like the others, she was forced to entertain customers or have her wages cut. "My first customer was a westerner in his 30s," she said with tears rolling down her cheeks. "It was scary and I really didn't like it, but I just kept thinking about the money. I couldn't wait for him to leave and when he did, I took a very long shower. I cried terribly, because it felt like I had not only sold my body, but my soul, too. What would my parents think if they found out what I was doing? What would I tell my daughter when she grew up?

One day, an adult film producer came to the bar looking for 'fresh talent'. He offered me a leading role in his 'new film'. I was excited over the prospects of becoming an actress, but knew little about what kind of film or role it was. When I went for my first shoot in the morning, he told me that it would be a group sex scene. They threatened me with dire consequences if I did not listen to them. Faced with limited options, I quietly agreed.

Everyday was just dreadful. I got up, dressed, put on make-up and nice clothes, only to remove them on the set. I acted in almost all categories of porn movies.

One morning, when I went to work thinking it was a normal scene, I was surprised to see 20 men of various ages waiting outside. When I went in, the director told me that these were the 20 new 'stars' with whom I would have to perform. I came to know that they were not actually male porn stars, but men who had been invited through an online advertisement to 'meet' a leading porn star for free.

"I cried and protested, while the director threatened. For some unfathomable reason, one of the men turned sympathetic and objected to what was happening. He saved me from that hell. That was the day I decided to quit. A friend then told me about Nightlights Christian charity, which offered skills training to rehabilitate former sex workers. It was there that I met Vijay Desai, one of the sponsors of the program. The rest is history. Now, my daughter is studying in a medical college and will one day become a successful doctor like you, John."

"Yes," I said. "A successful doctor like me, but not an unsuccessful investor. She will have the wealth of your wisdom to guide her onto the right path." This cheered up Duan.

My respect for that lady had multiplied several times over. I had no words to express it. She said, "the time has come for me to hand over Vijay's parcel to you." I noticed the envelope came with the memento of a home embossed on it. Exhorting me to read and digest the letter it contained, she disappeared indoors.

The Greatest Teachers of Life – Our Mistakes

Making common financial mistakes can destroy your home and impoverish your family

Don't throw good money after bad money, because money lost is money gone. Start afresh and don't ever base your financial decisions on the past. Don't compartmentalize losses and gains. Always consider money received from all sources as equally sacred. Many a time one is not able to make a decision and people often just go for maintaining the status quo. However, few realize that not making a decision is also a decision in itself that has consequences.

Selective thinking is a common, dangerous illusion that blocks the flow of all relevant information required for making the right financial decision. If you assume that saving is equal to investing, then you might be in for a big surprise. Bear in mind that income tax reduces your gross income. Interest on loans/bad capital assets diminishes your net income and inflation eats away the remaining income. The small things we forget while thinking big get compounded over a period of time to result in much bigger losses. It is a misconception that experts can beat the normal market indices. Be wary of becoming victim to either over-confidence or lack of confidence. Even completely rational people take irrational decisions when they are part of a crowd, surrendering to the low crowd mentality. Give equal respect to what belongs to you and others. Don't buy things you don't need, but don't be stingy, either. Even if you do become wealthy by being cheap, you will not be able to stay wealthy unless you spend and invest like a wealthy investor. Whether dealing with life or money, follow a plan and pursue it with moral courage, love and dedication. Learn from your mistakes. Train yourself to remain positive no matter how dire the circumstances. Follow this and your spirit will be lifted from the darkness of hell to the brightness of heaven, where you will find an abundance of life and money.

Insurance – Even a
Terrorist Needs It

As I waited at the airport in Thailand for my flight to Kabul, Afghanistan, I was overcome by the dread of landing in the land of the Taliban. But soon my mind went back to this remarkable woman I had met in Bangkok. Duan Aimond had taught me so much about life and money. Simply incredible. I realized why Vijay had made Duan the safekeeper of this piece of financial wisdom. Who better than the woman who had learned from her own and other's mistakes, lifting herself from the darkness of hell to the brightness of heaven. Although broken when very young, she had rebuilt a new, beautiful house on a solid foundation. She was the perfect symbol, a living example, of the wisdom she had imparted to me.

I wondered what my next destination held in store for me.

My flight was scheduled to leave at 5 pm and it was right on time. A beautiful young woman of about 25 occupied the seat next to me. As I admired her beauty, I remembered all those young girls on the streets of Bangkok waiting for their next customer, and cringed. Wonder what kind of a life she leads, I thought, and hoped it was nothing like what those girls suffered. I was surprised at myself. Before meeting Duan, I would have probably just thought, hmm, nice-looking! The kindness, character and moral values I had learned from Duan was paying off as a positive reflection on my overall character.

All they served on this flight was light snacks and coffee. I settled in for a nice nap thinking I would probably not be able to sleep peacefully in Kabul. I was woken by a soft voice urging me to make way. I realized I had slept through the entire flight. The plane had landed in Kabul. I yawned and stretched. My flight companion was now struggling to bring down her luggage from the overhead compartment. Helping her, I followed with my own luggage.

I arrived on the streets of Kabul at 7:30 pm.

As I looked around expecting some beefy Afghan to approach me, a gentle voice said, "good evening, Mr John Pinto. I am Fereshteh and I am here to collect you on behalf of Mr Feda Wahidi. He is the man chosen by Mr Vijay Desai to be with you in Kabul."

Fereshteh led me to a taxi, which looked nothing like a taxi. Acutely aware of the fact that I was in Afghanistan, I wondered if it was some kind of a police vehicle.

Fereshteh, clad in a typical hijab, began talking about Kabul. "It has a population of around 4,000,000 people and is located about 2,000 meters above sea level, making it one of the highest capital cities in the world. It is strategically located in a valley surrounded by high mountains at the crossroads of the north-south and east-west trade routes. It lies near the Khyber Pass, an important route between Afghanistan and

Pakistan. It is subject to extreme temperature changes, from night to day, season to season and place to place."

I nodded absent-mindedly.

My lessons in Kabul's history and geography continued as we slowly moved away from the main city and toward the mountains. The roads began to narrow and curve this way and that. My heart sank as I realized where I was being led. Oblivious to my growing anxiety, Fereshteh said calmly, "you will enjoy the beauty of these mountains."

It was about half an hour before the car came to an abrupt halt. Fereshteh stepped out and told me we would have to walk the rest of the way, indicating a mountain peak on the other side. I wondered whether it was just the other side or another world. I had no choice but to follow her. The mountains, now enveloped in darkness, looked even more menacing. As Fereshteh bent over to remove a torch from one of her socks, I noticed a gun sticking out of the other. Sensing my gaze, Fereshteh hastened to say, "don't worry, that is only for our protection."

Our protection or my execution, I wondered.

After what felt like ages of climbing by the light of a torch, I finally saw the top of a big stone house. There appeared to be some kind of a tunnel opposite the house and small hideouts on either side of it. Now, I was convinced this was a terrorist hideout. But realizing that I was at a point of no return, I walked straight toward what appeared like a house of death to me.

We were greeted by a tall, muscular man clad in the typical Pashtun dress of a loose-fitting salwar kameez and turban. As he embraced me in a vice-like grip, I felt like a sheep about to be slaughtered.

"Welcome, Mr John Pinto. I am Feda Wahidi."

"Thank you, sir."

I hesitated at the threshold of his house. Its floors were covered in stylishly patterned carpets, the brocade sofas adorned with brightly colored pillows and the walls tastefully appointed with framed pictures of birds and flowers. There I also saw rifles, pistols and knives. My heart skipped a beat as Feda Wahidi ushered me in.

"Oh, man," announced Feda. "Don't be afraid. I use these weapons for our protection, although at one point, I used it for mass destruction."

What?

He quickly added, "I used to be a terrorist. Vijay and his financial commandments changed me. I now use my powers for the safety and betterment of humanity."

I felt somewhat relieved. If my friend, Vijay, and his financial wisdom had inspired Duan, a prostitute, it could have well inspired a terrorist like Feda to also change his life.

"Let me have the pleasure of offering you the best food of Kabul," Feda's words interrupted my thoughts.

"Come on, friend," Feda led me to a large, wooden dining table in the other room.

"Let's start with the *shorma*," he said, ladling out a big helping of the warm Afghan soup. The intense aroma made my mouth water and considerably eased the tension I had been feeling until then. Where else was I going to enjoy such authentic Afghan food if not in the mountains of Kabul! I picked up my spoon with enthusiasm. The soup was followed by kebabs, korma (a dish of fried onions and meat, mixed with fruits, spices and vegetables) *ashak* (a Kabul specialty), *obi* naan (shaped like a disk and thicker than the usual naan) and *chalow* (fluffy white rice). The food that night seemed out of this world!

Now that the edge had been taken off our appetites, we settled comfortably to talk. Feda served me that divine Afhgani pudding called *firnee* and brought the discussion round to finances. "Do you have a personal insurance policy?" he asked.

I took in a spoonful of the dessert, savoring the flavors of rosewater, cardamom and pistachios before saying, "no. Why do I need insurance? I earn well with my medical practice. Why waste money on insurance?"

Given the bizarre setting of this conversation and my lingering doubts, I suddenly forgot all about the *firnee* and started thinking that maybe this man is going to kill me and that's why he wants to know if I have an insurance policy.

"What if, God forbid, you had an accident and lost your limbs or were injured and unable to go to your clinic for two months? What if I shot you right here? Did you think before making this unknown journey around the world about what would happen to your family if you never returned?"

I was abashed. Indeed, I had never thought about this. For the first time since meeting Feda, my mind was fixated on something other than his bullet. I did not fear for my life but for what would happen to my family after me – my aged mother, my caring wife and my innocent children.

"Have you ever thought about how your family will live without you?" asked Feda hitting the nail on the head. "More than mourning your death, they will curse you for leaving them in a dire financial state. I believe you want people to love and respect you the same way after your death as they do today, right?"

I nodded.

"Then you have to respect their financial independence not only when you are alive, but even when you have left this world."

"But it's difficult to digest the idea of parting with my money for nothing. I mean, it's not as if something is going to happen to me every day."

"Something is going to happen to you someday and that day could be today; and when that something happens and you lose your life, then nothing is going to remain except your investment assets and insurance money," Feda retorted.

"Nobody wants to just give away something for nothing. Everyone is looking for a return. If you love somebody, you want love in return; if you respect somebody, you want respect in return and so on. The same psychology explains why people go for insurance policies that return something on maturity. One thing you have to bear in mind, John, is that insurance is, indeed, either getting everything or nothing for something. In the event of a catastrophe, you will get the full sum assured as an insurance cover, and if it doesn't happen, you'll get nothing.

If you think that you should get something in return even if nothing happens, then you are making a grave financial mistake. This is because insurers are very bad money managers. Their costs are very high and the return after such costs and money management is very poor."

Indeed, I remembered how a few years ago I was lured into buying one such *money back policy*. I did get my money back, but the return on it was abysmally low – I earned just 6.5% per annum, when the normal return on long-term debt at that time was around 10% per annum. So, I had paid around 3.5% per annum in under performance, when I could have purchased the equivalent policy cover for just 0.5% per annum and earned the remaining 10% from long-term debt, giving me a clear extra 3% per annum. What a foolish thing I had done, combining insurance with investment.

Revelling in my newfound wisdom, I said, "yes Feda, hoping to get something besides the policy cover from insurance is foolishness."

Excited that I had understood him so quickly, he elaborated his point. "Many people see insurance as an investment vehicle. But insurance is not investment, otherwise why would there be two different financial products? Never combine investments with insurance. Don't forget that insurance is always bad investment and that investments should not provide you with insurance. You invest money for earning returns, whereas you take insurance to protect yourself against untoward events. Take pure insurance in the form of a term policy. This advice may be contrary to what most financial planners and experts will give, because the commission on a pure term policy is the minimum. The fact that the commission is the least on term policy is further proof that the insurance company believes it to be the best product, incurring the lowest expenses. The insurance company's earnings from it are the least and therefore, it isn't deemed worthwhile to promote it."

Here was a former militant giving me better advice than the most experienced professional financial planners or advisors.

"There is one more facet to insurance and that is the insurance money," Feda continued.

"This is another important aspect that generally nobody thinks about. Every advisor will talk about which policy to take, but nobody advises you on what to do with the insurance money. Say, you are an unfortunate young widow who inherits a reasonable sum in insurance. There will be plenty of so-called financial planners and advisors after you to sell you the next hot investment product with an eye on your newly found wealth in the form of the insurance money.

I regret to say that these advisors are worse than terrorists. They pounce on the money of the dead. And if the surviving partner has never handled finances in his life, he's definitely in for a nightmare."

"So what should one do in such a situation," I asked befuddled.

"Just stay calm as you try to come out of the trauma of losing your better half. Simply put that sum in a money market, liquid mutual fund scheme or lock it into a short-term, say a fixed three-month bank deposit. This will give you enough time to overcome the trauma and take an informed decision. Also, it will give you time to figure out if there are any liabilities of your deceased partner left to be paid, so you can take care of those first. Once you have crossed the initial stage, understood your partner's estate, liabilities, tax status, etc., make a proper asset allocation plan. If your partner has left behind a ready-made plan, then just assess, review and appraise the plan and make any necessary changes, including the insurance amounts, if any, to bring it in line with your asset allocation plan."

This made a lot of sense. How could anyone see money received from the insurance company as his newfound wealth? Only if people fall victim to *mental accounting* (the concept I learned from Duan) were they likely to squander away the insurance money or hand it over to financial advisors, who charge high fees for providing sub-standard investment advice. I realized with a start that I was connecting the advice from Feda with what I had learned from Duan.

"But how does one draw up a proper asset allocation plan?" I asked Feda with great interest.

"That will be revealed to you by someone else," he replied mysteriously, reminding me that it was time to call it a day so we could be up early for our patrol the next morning.

However, worries over the implications of not taking appropriate insurance before embarking on this dangerous, adventurous and unknown world tour kept me wide awake in bed most of the night.

I awoke the next morning to the chirping of birds and a young girl who was drawing back the curtains.

"We Afghans believe the morning sun is sacred and should be allowed to enter the house. If you wake up late in the morning, you are stealing important hours from your own life."

Her words went straight to my heart. I wondered how many costly hours of my life I had stolen because of my habit of getting up late.

I freshened up and headed straight to the dining room, where Feda was having his morning tea. "We Afghans simply love our morning tea," he said. "It is called *qiamaq* chai, or green tea that is put through a series of aerations and treated with baking soda till it turns dark red. It goes best with the *roht* (a round, sweet flat bread), my favorite. And I enjoy my breakfast while listening to the birds over here."

Feda urged me to hurry up with my breakfast, reminding me that we had to go on patrol. We made our way through the mountains in a jeep that looked like a police vehicle.

I couldn't help being sarcastic, "so even militants use police cars over here."

Feda kept his cool. "I am a police informer."

"What?" I gasped.

"Yes. I used to be a terrorist, but as I told you earlier, Vijay changed my life. I now act as the eyes and ears of the police and report any suspicious activities in and around this region."

As we drove around the mountains, Feda pointed out places where he had carried out his terrorist activities. He recounted how he had cruelly taken so many lives, heartlessly slaughtering a son in front of his mother, a husband in front of his wife, a young daughter in front of her father. Soon his voice became brittle with remorse. I waited till he regained some composure and asked, "what drove you to terrorism in the first place?"

"I was the only son of a rich Kabul trader. But my father met with an accident and died. Since he was very rich, he hadn't seen any reason to take insurance. To make things worse, he suffered too much debt from the negative leverage he used to buy bad capital assets along with a number of speculative items. Neither did he protect his money from financial predators, nor did he budget for himself and his family.

My mother could not take care of her husband's complex, unprotected and debt-ridden business empire. So, it collapsed like a pack of cards, leaving the family buried under a mountain of debt. Unable to bear the burden and the humiliation of it all, my mother died shortly afterward. I, too, grew tired of listening to the constant taunting and, being young and vulnerable, fell prey to the militants' call for jihad."

His killing spree eventually landed him in jail. And it was there that he met Vijay, who had been invited as a guest speaker. Vijay's talk on the rules of life and money influenced his thoughts to such an extent that he vowed never to return to his old ways. His sincerity convinced the authorities that he could be used as an informer, thereby earning him clemency for his former crimes.

Feda remained in touch with Vijay through the years. Vijay, too, visited him to help him through his first few days as a free man.

What a noble soul my friend was! I remembered how at the age of 15, he used to tell us that our thoughts and actions define who we are: "As we think, so we do. All our thoughts have great vibrations. If we think positively, we send positive vibrations into our surroundings, which then bounce back to us. Only when we are kind to others, can we be kind to ourselves; only when we think well of others, can we be good to ourselves; and only if we love others, can we love ourselves. When we educate others, our own knowledge increases; when we help others become rich, we too become wealthy."

"My father's business and estate bled only because of the lack of legal and tax insurance policies," Feda added. These terms were new to me.

Feda grinned and explained, "there are a number of rogues around the world, who know how to rob you of your money legally. Remember, there are thousands of people out there waiting for an excuse to use a lawsuit to become rich. There are lawyers who actually specialize in these kinds of cases."

I knew well the truth of this statement. Many years ago, a fraudulent suit was brought against me for an operation I had conducted. I had been forced to cough up a small fortune to settle and had almost become bankrupt paying that sum. Even now, I'm still in debt for it. As though reading my thoughts, Feda said, "you need legal insurance, my friend."

"I have studied different insurance policies offered by almost all the insurance companies. I am not aware of anyone offering legal insurance," I said.

He laughed. "Just as God is not visible to the naked eye and can only be felt with one's heart and soul, so, too, are many of the important financial answers not readily available. They are waiting to be explored by those who are financially savvy."

On being pressed to reveal more, he said, "first, don't keep assets of much value in your personal name. Hold assets in good legal entities, such as a company, limited liability partnership or trust. These not only help secure your assets by separating you as an individual from your asset, but also provide it with perpetual succession. Therefore, your asset is protected not only throughout your life, but also after you have left this world. You need to take personal liability insurance, which is a kind of risk financing to protect the purchaser from the risks of liabilities arising from lawsuits and other similar claims. It protects the insured in the event he is sued for claims that come under the cover of the insurance policy. And finally, prepare your counter attack by having your own legal attorney."

I suddenly understood why rich people like Vijay owned their assets not in their personal names, but in the names of their companies.

Feda continued, "you must also take tax insurance, because the government is the biggest legal financial predator. It legally and systematically takes away money from your pocket at every stage. Therefore, you have to learn to earn the most tax-efficient income, like portfolio or passive income, as opposed to earned or guaranteed income. You must save on tax by spending out of pre-tax, not post-tax, income. You must protect yourself from various indirect taxes such as sales tax, service tax, excise duty, customs duty, etc., at the time of spending. Furthermore, you must save tax at the time of investing and insuring as there are different taxes, such as a securities transaction tax, levied at this stage. You may take the help of a tax consultant if you are not properly conversant with the tax laws."

"But these legal and tax advisors are so costly," I protested. "How can someone like me afford them?"

"That's a common problem," Feda responded, "with no easy answers. But I'll try to resolve your dilemma. You're a specialist commanding high fees for your services. However, there are many young budding doctors with less experience, but with the knowledge and enthusiasm to work. The key is to find those professionals who are students of their own professions."

Why had I not thought of that? So many young doctors trained under me. It would have cost many of my patients a fraction of what it costs to be treated by me, while receiving the same quality of treatment. It also would have been quicker.

"You know, many of the terrorists in this region have personal insurance," Feda told me much to my astonishment.

Toward the end of our patrol, we headed back to Feda's house on the other side of the mountain. I was now beginning to enjoy traveling on those mountainous roads.

Delectable Afghan delicacies awaited us. After a heavy supper, I relaxed in my room. Feda told me we would spend the rest of the evening making his routine reports to the police. From my window I could see the stunning sunset over the mountains. After a heavy Afghan feast at night, to which my tummy was now getting habituated, I drifted off to sleep in these blissful surroundings.

I was excited the next morning at the thought of visiting Kabul city. I had read about its many renowned museums, gardens and mosques. Feda drove us into the city after a sumptuous breakfast and his favorite morning cuppa. He gave me a quick summary of the city's most famous sights, such as the Afghan National Museum, Kabul Zoo, Bagh-e-Zanana, Babur Gardens, Bagh-e Bala and Darul Aman Palace.

His descriptions whet my curiosity and I couldn't wait to see them. But my enthusiasm evaporated when he told me we would not be going to any of those iconic places.

"We will first go to the city hospital to keep my appointment with my doctor friend, and then proceed to the High Court to meet a lawyer and then finally, the central Kabul market."

We headed to the hospital, where he introduced me to Dr. Zalmai. As it turned out, this doctor used to work at the terrorists' camps, but had turned over a new leaf like Feda.

The doctor led us to where his patients lay. "You see that man over there," the doctor pointed to a man of about 50 with just one leg. "He used to work as a driver. One day, he suffered a car accident. He had to have one leg amputated. He had neither personal insurance, nor a medical policy or any kind of disability protection. He not only lost his income-earning capacity, but without mediclaim, he could not pay his hospital bills and without disability protection, there was nothing to compensate for his lack of income. It is only because of Feda's help, that he and his family are still surviving."

Not only did this man lose his earnings and was unable to pay his medical bills, but his son had to quit college and start working . His daughter also had to forego her higher studies and get married at a tender young age. His mental and physical anguish was clearly written over his face.

Next, we headed to the High Court to meet the lawyer. But I could not get that poor man in the hospital out of my mind. Sensing my sadness, Feda advised, "taking insurance is an absolute necessity – personal insurance to protect your family in the event of your death, and disability insurance to protect them, as well as yourself, in the event of losing your income-earning capacity."

By this time, we had reached the gates of the High Court. Feda took me directly to the cabin of Mr Mehrang, one of the city's top lawyers. Feda spoke to him about a friend whose car was involved in a minor accident. A dubious lawsuit had been brought against him, seeking an obscene amount in damages. Mr Mehrang had taken up the case at the behest of Feda after a lower court had ruled in favor of the prosecution. I understood from their conversation that Feda's friend's reputation was in tatters and his family had all but been reduced to living on the streets.

As we headed back to the car, we passed the courtroom. Feda paused outside it and turning to me said, "this is where the legal sharks sit. They are ready to pounce on you and drain you of your money and happiness. Always take third party insurance to protect yourself from dubious lawsuits. One such shark has nearly ruined my friend."

"But how can somebody do that," I protested angrily.

"By taking advantage of loopholes in the law. Therefore, whether driving a car, running a factory or operating on a patient, don't forget to subscribe to third party insurance."

That explains what happened to one of my friends years ago, I thought. He had lost his license to practice medicine after being falsely accused of professional misconduct and negligence by a female patient with her own selfish motives. The legal costs of fighting his case had almost left him bankrupted as he had to borrow money at high interest rates. To this day, he is working hard in the hospital at a low level clerical position to just pay off that debt. Feda was right, the legal sharks.

We then drove to the city market. After shopping for meat, groceries and vegetables, we headed toward the fruit market. Feda told me that his friend sold some of the best fresh fruits grown in Afghanistan: grapes, pomegranates, berries, apricots, oranges, plums and more. Feda picked some of the finest fruits at this man's stall and the vendor only very reluctantly accepted payment for it. He also treated us to deliciously fresh pomegranate juice.

On returning to Feda's house, I asked him why the fruit vendor was so reluctant to accept cash. Feda laughed and said, "that's because I saved him from ending up on the streets by helping him set up this fruit business.

He once ran a transport business. His trucks delivered fresh fruit to all corners of the country from the farms. However, he was guilty of a grave mistake. To save money on insurance, he didn't insure his vehicles. One day, one of his vehicles overturned while speeding on the highway and the driver lost his life. When the police discovered that his vehicle wasn't insured, he not only lost his business license, but also became subject to heavy fines. He lost the trust of his clients and everyone began to avoid him, viewing him as a criminal. But I have known him for a long time. He was no criminal, just foolish, penny-wise and pound-foolish. I helped him set up this fruit stall. Now, I believe, even his fruits are insured," Feda laughed aloud at his own joke.

Feda then told me that we would be joined by an old friend of his for dinner that evening. I knew that this would be another opportunity to become financially wiser.

The evening came and so did Feda's friend. I was introduced to Mr Omaid, a grocer in central Kabul. From the conversation between him and Feda, I realized he knew a great deal about automobile parts and components.

So why was this man running a grocery store?

Omaid's eyes overflowed with tears when he heard my question. He was speechless. Feda volunteered to break the tense silence and resolve the mystery himself.

"Omaid had one of the best automobile parts and components factories in Afghanistan. But he lost everything overnight when a fire gutted his factory. He lost the machines, the raw material, products, walls, roof – everything."

"Oh my God!" I exclaimed. "Didn't he have insurance?"

"He did have the normal fire cover, but not loss of profit cover."

Now what was that?

"Insuring one's property, buildings, fixtures and fittings, stock and equipment are obviously important, but so is the need for adequate cover for loss of profit following loss or damage at one's premises. Business interruptions do happen! Apart from the direct losses that arise from a fire, there are also losses that result from the interruption of a business. If damage to one's business premises forces it to close down pending repairs, employees will still have to be paid, mortgages, leases and other debts as well. These expenses can mount up quickly for a business that has reduced or no income. So, this policy could act as a vital lifeline for businesses. And my good friend, Omaid, did not have this vital lifeline."

"So a loss of profit pays for the business bills while the business is temporarily disabled and not running," I said armed with my newly gained knowledge.

"Excellent!" Feda shouted in delight. "So you're picking up my language, John, the language of insurance and protection. My friend, Omaid, didn't have that kind of insurance. His business bills like salaries, bank interest, mortgages, leases and other debts kept mounting, but he couldn't pay. He was tragically forced to wind up his business."

Sweeping changes in the international political landscape and widespread market deregulation have made trade the driving force in the world economy. But expanding sales and building new customer relationships can expose people to heightened credit risks. Economic downturns can leave customers unable to pay what they owe. And often, it's too late by the time one comes to know of a customer's insolvency. Therefore, this also requires insurance protection. The insurance policy which protects against customer insolvency is known as *credit insurance*. Omaid didn't have this either."

I instantly realized the importance of credit insurance when I remembered how many times my patients had delayed paying me my fees on some pretext or other. Feda's words were worth their weight in millions of dollars to the person who understood and accepted them.

As usual, our dinner ended with delicious mouth-watering sweets, desserts, fruit and coffee. I took leave of Omaid and Feda, but stayed awake for a long time that night. All the various categories of insurance kept coming back to me – family protection, personal insurance, disability protection, third party insurance, vehicle insurance, loss of profit protection and credit insurance. I also thought how apt the expression 'penny-wise and pound-foolish' was to describe the actions of one who would not take insurance to save some money on the insurance premium, risking their entire family's financial security in the process.

The next morning at breakfast, gulping down his favorite tea, Feda told me he was now ready to hand over the nugget of financial wisdom for which Vijay had sent me to this desolate mountainous region.

I could hardly wait for it. I started drinking my tea with a sense of purpose now. As I rushed through tea and breakfast, Feda smiled and finally extended an envelope and a small memento with a picture of a soldier on it.

The License to Live Your Life

Just as a soldier protects his country from all enemy attacks, insurance protects you, your family, assets and business against all kinds of attacks.

Financial education is incomplete without financial insurance. Just as daily exercise is insurance against future health problems, the right policy is insurance against future financial losses. It would not be possible to earn, budget, protect, save, spend, leverage or invest to one's full potential without it. The major categories of financial insurance include family protection, disability protection, asset protection, loss of profit protection, personal insurance and medical insurance. There are other categories that protect one's wealth from money predators. These include legal insurance (protection against legal rogues), tax insurance (protection against the government taxmen), competitor protection (to be able to remain in the business in which one is today), love protection (those who pretend to love for selfish ulterior motives) and portfolio insurance (to protect one's assets against unexpected large losses). Look for details in your life to know which policy suits you best.

You are throwing away valuable hours of your own life if you have a terrible habit of getting up late in the morning. Similarly, you are robbing yourself of your own money when you delay taking the appropriate insurance policy for yourself. Don't expect something in return for your money except the protection which it intends to provide you with. Also, never combine investments with insurance, since insurance is always bad investment and investments do not provide insurance. Acquaint yourself with how to take care of your newfound wealth in the form of insurance money by following the financial commandments and their wisdom. Insure your relationships with others by treating them well on your way up so that they will be encouraged to treat you well when you are down. Being kind to others will allow you to be kind to yourself, ensuring you subscribe to the correct insurance policy. The appropriate insurance policy is your license to enjoy life to the fullest.

Mystics and Money Creation

I wished Feda Wahidi goodbye with a heavy heart. My stay with him had been most enlightening. He had taught me the importance of insurance or, more specifically, financial insurance.

This was the fifth day of my incredible journey around the world. Feda informed me that my next destination was Zhujiajiao, a water town near Shanghai, where I would meet my new guru – a Chinese woman of just 25. I had never been to China, the most populous country in the world. I had, however, read a lot about its people, culture, growing military prowess and, of course, its recent financial and economic success. I was aware of how China had become the new driving force, the engine of global growth. And I was set to receive financial wisdom from a young Chinese woman. It certainly promised to be exciting and I was feeling far less anxious than when I was flying into Afghanistan.

I had taken the 8 am flight from Kabul to Shanghai.

The local time when I arrived was 4.30 pm. My life had moved ahead by three and a half hours. By now, I was acutely aware of time and its importance.

As I waited outside the busy Shanghai airport bursting with the sound of cars, buses and other vehicles, a beautiful young lady with long hair came up to me. In fluent English she asked, "Mr John Pinto? I am Faline Cheong. I have been assigned by your friend to share the fourth nugget of financial wisdom with you." I replied with the default Chinese greeting *Ni Hao* to impress the young lady.

I couldn't help admiring her glowing skin, long black hair and enchanting eyes. She was wearing loose clothes with large sleeves, and embroidered, heeled clogs. Her arm was wrapped in a scarf, which I later learned was called *jinguo*.

"We are heading toward Zhujiajiao, my hometown," Faline said in an authoritative, but sweet voice. Something about her face, voice and behavior left me feeling that I was in the presence of an enigmatic personality.

"It will take around one and a half hours to get there, and then a short boat trip to my house," Faline continued.

I kept nodding as the cab wove its way in and out of the fast-moving Shanghai traffic. I marveled at China's superb infrastructure and couldn't help comparing it with India's. Today, China is the largest consumer of most natural resources and metals, such as steel, copper, aluminum, zinc, etc., and is home to some of the most beautiful cities, roads, towers, ports and airports.

"Yes, China has made very good progress on infrastructure, because of government policies and positive leverage," she said as though reading my mind. When asked about it, she answered, "it's the leverage of clairaudience."

I was began to worry. Clairaudience, I knew, is the power to hear sounds that exist beyond the reach of ordinary human capacity. That means she had the ability to read my mind, to know what thoughts were going through my head.

"Don't stress your brain too much, John," she said suddenly. "You will understand everything slowly."

My mind started working overtime. What would I come to understand? Who was she? What kind of powers did she have? How was she able to read me like an open book?

Faline grinned as I tried hard to suppress my thoughts.

I was in a water town with a young woman almost half my age, who had the astonishing ability to read my mind. This visit may not turn out to be the way I had imagined it.

"Be calm and patient," Faline said softly holding my hands in hers. "Everything is, and will be, fine. Don't think too much. Life is uncertain and has its ups and downs. There is risk in everything: to love is to risk not having it reciprocated; to speak is to risk not being listened to; to work is to risk being unappreciated. But, if we don't move through this uncertain environment by conquering our fears and taking calculated risks, we're not going to progress in life, financially and otherwise. You should learn to take risks in life by doing what you fear. You should take risks while dealing with money, but in line with the ten financial commandments. You should learn to harness the power of positive leverage so as to multiply your money and wealth. And never try to over-leverage, whether dealing with your life or your money, because greed is a great enemy of men."

In just a couple of minutes, Faline had shared a wealth of knowledge on life and money with me. She had opened up my mind by showing me a new perspective on uncertainty, risk, fear, worry, greed and something else – leverage.

What was this leverage?

"Leverage is the power of multiplication," she said before I could even frame the question. But it didn't throw me off. I was slowly getting used to receiving answers to questions that had just popped into in my head.

"It is a simple concept that basically says money in your hands is worth more than money in your neighbor's hands. Leverage simply puts your neighbor's money into your hands. And once it comes into your hands, you can invest with that money. So, you earn on money that you originally did not own."

Seeing me baffled, Faline smiled broadly and continued, "leverage helps you buy an investment asset with somebody else's money. You keep the income and the asset with you. Once your loan and interest are repaid, your investment asset keeps working for you all your life. You get money for practically nothing, creating money out thin air. It's almost as if you've printed your own money. That's the power of positive leverage."

Creating money out of thin air and printing my own money? This sure was exciting.

"Yes," Faline affirmed. "Look at the driver of this cab. He isn't just a driver. He is the owner of ten such cars, which ply in and around Shanghai. He runs a tourism transport business. He used to be just a driver, but when he understood the power of positive leverage, he used debt to his own advantage. He leveraged his savings and borrowed the maximum permissible to invest in a cab. The income from the cab paid off his debt and then the income from that cab was free for life. This was money he had printed off somebody else – the bank. He borrowed against that money to create further positive leverage. Today, he is the proud owner of a fleet of ten tourist cars."

On reaching Zhujiajiao, we got out of the car and into a boat. Our boat passed under an old bridge across bubbling streams and small rivers shaded by willow trees.

"This is just one of the 36 bridges. Zhujiajiao is an ancient water town of more than 1,700 years old."

I marveled at her knowledge of her hometown. As usual, she had read my mind.

"This is called the leverage of knowledge. Leverage is not just about money. After all, what is money? It's nothing but currency and its value is compromised every day due to inflation. Over the long-term, the money that you hold is going to be worth less and less, because inflation will erode its purchasing power at a rapid pace.

The only thing which will stand you in good stead in this modern age of money, finance and currency is your financial knowledge. It is your knowledge of dealing with money at every stage that will give you financial independence. And so, you've been sent on this incredible journey by your friend, Vijay Desai, to acquaint yourself with the financial commandments. Their wisdom will unleash the leverage of your own mind. Be aware that the biggest leverage that all human beings possess is financial knowledge. Therefore, strengthen this leverage and you'll be able to unleash the power within you to expand the boundaries of wealth and happiness. Once you're able to do this, you can say you have mastered the financial wisdom for which you have been sent here to meet me in China."

We soon reached Faline's home. I stepped off the boat gingerly and entered the house through an ornate door. Her house was beautifully furnished with a balance of old and new furniture. The floors were covered with classically patterned carpets, the sofa adorned with vibrantly colored pillows, the walls plastered with tastefully framed pictures of rivers and boats. One thing that stood out were the many lit candles around the house. She also had many *diyas* (the touch glass filled with oil and then lit) in all corners of the house.

The clock hanging on the wall indicated that it was 6 pm. Faline offered me a glass of water and said, "say a short prayer before you have this water. This is pure prayer water. Make yourself comfortable as I offer my evening prayers before the sun sets."

I did as instructed. The water tasted heavenly. It not only quenched my thirst, but also made me feel relaxed. As the day's tensions began to melt, my mind went back to all the silk scarves, mosaic lamps and the multi-colored jewelry I had seen as we traveled through Zhujiajiao to Faline's house by boat. I remembered how my wife loves wearing brightly colored scarves and jewelry, but I could never afford anything decent for her. And she had never once complained, neither about the lack of gifts, nor about the financial and money mistakes I had made all along.

In just two hours with Faline, I had learned so many things about conquering fear, replacing uncertainty with proper direction, reducing risk with knowledge, not worrying unnecessarily about things beyond one's control and replacing greed with positive financial leverage.

After about half an hour, Faline returned and said that she was done with her evening prayers.

"So how many times in a day do you pray, Faline?"

"It's not how many times you pray that is important. It's with what faith and dedication that you pray that is imperative. It's how you follow God's commandments that's important. Similarly, in the financial world, how you accept and comply with the financial commandments is what's important.

The most powerful prayer is the prayer for the spiritual growth of another being. Some people pray to show off, others to prove that they are truly pious. Prayers should be short and sweet. They should be full of feelings that are positive, genuine and totally selfless."

Taking a sip of the prayer water, she continued, "in the money world, the most important thing is to follow the financial commandments and their wisdom to enhance your own wealth and then, bequeath it to the next generation and give to charity. Charity should be done silently and selflessly, sans any ulterior motive or expectations of return."

Both prayer and charity should be quiet, selfless and without any ulterior motive. The financial commandments were in unity with God's commandments, I thought.

"If you pray sincerely for yourself and other living creatures," Faline added, "if you're on the right path and it doesn't interfere with your karma, then it's sure to be answered. The same way, if you're on the right financial path and make wise financial decisions, your financial growth is bound to happen."

The only thing I didn't understand here was this new word 'karma'.

Again reading my mind, Faline said, "karma is the positive credit or the negative debit, that a soul has accumulated through its good or bad deeds. Every soul has to pay back its negative karmic debt. The soul is also rewarded for its positive karma in the form of special qualities like singing, acting, speaking, writing, etc., the same way that you are a good doctor. As you create positive and negative karma with your deeds, you also create positive and negative leverage while dealing with debt. Therefore, always create positive karma or leverage."

"And what if we don't know the difference between positive or negative karma or leverage?"

"Your prayer will yield positive karma for your spiritual growth, while the knowledge of the financial commandments will lead you to positive leverage for your financial growth."

"But," I persisted in testing her faith, "what do you gain by prayer and meditation?"

"Maybe nothing. But I have rid myself of anger, fear and depression."

Ignoring my puzzled look, she continued, "no matter what our earthly wealth and possessions, peace of mind can only be attained by staying on God's path. When we go through ups and downs in life, prayer helps us remain calm. This is important when one is faced with a calamity. You must not allow a problem to crush you, nor must you let success go to your head.

Pride is the biggest enemy of every human being, especially while dealing with money. Why do you think so many people lose money in the stock markets or take up negative leverage and end up bankrupt? Because of pride. So whenever you achieve something, money wise or otherwise, don't feel great, be grateful."

I was astonished at the knowledge, understanding and maturity of this 25-year-old woman. How much of the world could she have seen in her 25 years living in this small water town?

Reading my mind as usual, she answered, "we aren't human beings. We are spirits."

What? The only spirit I was familiar with was the liquor I drank.

"This is a serious matter," she said with a mystical look. "Let me ask you, John, who are you? Where have you come from? Why does one live a finite life on this planet and one day die? Where does one go when one dies? Do you have the answers to these questions?"

"No," came my reply.

"That's because we're all spirits. We occupy this physical body because of our karma. And once our objective of coming to the world is met, we return to our real home – the spirit world."

That sounded scary, but logical all the same. We do come from somewhere and live in this world for a finite time as death is certain for one and all.

By now the sun had set and as I looked out of the window, I saw a gibbous moon flaunting its bold face.

"So, what else do you know about us humans – sorry, spirits?"

"Maybe a lot or maybe very little. But this isn't the time to talk about all that. I promise you I'll educate you on human beings, or rather spirits, as well as money before you leave Zhujiajiao. But for now, I think you should relax and get ready for dinner."

I was taken to an adjoining room, which was the dining room. It had beautiful hanging lights, a window at one end and a door at the other that opened into the kitchen. The dining table, funnily enough, stood on a foot-high wooden platform. The table itself was also made of wood and its light brown polish nicely complemented the comfortable-looking chairs.

As we sat for dinner, Faline closed her eyes and recited a small prayer. "We should always remember our creator before eating what He has made for us."

We were first served Chinese corn and cabbage soup. It was a clear, hot soup with plenty of corn, cabbage and mushrooms. The table soon filled up with the main course, comprising authentic Chinese delicacies such as drunken chicken, *char siu*, General Tso's chicken, Yunnan goat cheese with *dandan* noodles and basil fried rice. The dessert was a surprising cookie called Earl Grey Shortbread, which was something like a peanut butter cookie.

While enjoying dessert, I was seized with a sudden doubt.

"Faline, you're such a nice woman who believes in God. But then, isn't eating non-vegetarian food a sin?"

She took a deep breath and said, "why do you eat food? To live. Can you eat rock or sand? No, because they don't have life in them. Food gives you life and to give you life, it should itself have life. Therefore, whatever you eat, whether plants, vegetables, fruits or animals and fish, have life in them and so, give you life. This is God's rule. So, in my view, there's no harm in eating non-vegetarian food."

I had read and heard numerous arguments for and against non-vegetarianism, but never anything like this: What has life gives you life.

But Faline was not done. "Similarly, money gives you money. Your investment asset earns more money for you in the form of guaranteed, passive or portfolio income. And when you create positive leverage on your investment asset, it just multiplies your money."

I remembered that Vijay had said when your money works for you in the form of a bank deposit earning interest or equity stock earning dividend or rental real estate earning rent, then it is your money working for you, earning you guaranteed or passive income. And when someday, you sell and realize a profit from an investment asset that has appreciated in value during your holding period, you acquire portfolio income.

Faline, fully aware of what was going on in my head, said, "good, John, you should now settle down for the night, thinking about Vijay's wisdom." Bidding me good night, she disappeared into her bedroom.

It was a few more minutes before I drifted off to sleep, thinking about Faline Cheong in this unbelievable water town; about creating positive leverage through debt by investing in guaranteed, passive or portfolio income, generating investment assets and multiplying my own wealth... and about humans as spirits.

I was up early the next morning. The clock showed it was 6 am. The thought of robbing myself of my own life had, perhaps, started working on me. I went into the living room to find Faline reading a book. She told me that dawn is the best time of the day to start one's work. "Just as the sun rises from the depths of the universe, so does one's mind and thoughts emerge fresh from the depths of the dark night," she said.

Very soon, I was served with chrysanthemum tea (herbal tea). It was served in a big glass teapot. Chinese teas are usually herbal brews made from flowers, herbs, fruits and grains. This mellow tea came lightly sweetened with a cube of *bingtang*, or rock sugar. For breakfast, we had *zongzi* (a pyramid-shaped snack of sticky rice wrapped in bamboo or reed leaves) and crullers (deep-fried devils).

As we sat enjoying our morning tea and breakfast quietly, a man's voice broke the silence. We went to the door and saw a couple carrying an entire market with them in a large boat – vegetables, fruits, groceries, meat, chicken, fish, etc. Faline purchased quite a few items from them.

Once indoors, she told me, "this couple now owns their own boat and is earning handsomely by selling all kinds of food items. They once used to work as domestic help in other people's houses – washing clothes, utensils and cleaning the floors. They used to work for me, too. That's when I introduced them to the power of positive leverage. I explained how they could create an investment asset through positive leverage that would then multiply their gains."

Cleaners becoming merchants! This was beginning to sound interesting.

Faline had more to share. "I told them how they could borrow for comparatively low rates against the mortgage of their house and then buy the boat that would be their investment asset. Then, they could invest in items like vegetables and fruits. With a little courage, hard work and the backing and knowledge of the financial commandments, they turned from sweepers to entrepreneurs."

Why had I not done that? Instead, I had just blown up borrowed money by going in for unnecessary purchases.

"Yes, you have indeed blown up your money," Faline said. "People often do just that. They borrow money for all the wrong items, such as a car, expensive furniture, luxury items, costly holidays, etc. The irony of the fact is that, because of our faulty accounting principles, they consider them as assets when, in fact, they're nothing but pure cash-guzzling liabilities – liabilities disguised as accounting assets."

Cash-guzzling liabilities disguised as accounting assets?

"Yeah," she replied. "Let me explain. Cash-guzzling liabilities are like the expensive car you own: it takes money out of your pocket at the time of purchase by putting you into mortgage debt; at the time of using by recurring petrol expenses; and at the time of maintenance for costly spare parts. Also, since you own such a gruesome capital asset, you have to spend money insuring it. Remember Feda Wahidi of Afghanistan?"

How could I forget Feda Wahidi? After all, I had such a great time with him. But here, in this water town of Zhujiajiao, I was learning equally important principles of money, debt, leverage, assets and flaws in the traditional accounting system. But what was this gruesome capital asset?

No sooner had the doubt entered my mind, when Faline answered, "gruesome and bad capital assets, as well as unnecessary revenue expenditure, are not the terms you'll find in a traditional accounting textbook. Gruesome capital assets would mean those assets that produce negative income or empty your pocket, such as a car, beach house, etc. Bad capital assets would include those assets that don't give you any income, such as a self-occupied house. Unnecessary revenue expenditure would mean foreign trips, costly dinners and the like, that will just loot you."

As a doctor, I counted many accounting professionals among my patients, but I am sure I would have been hard-pressed to find someone who could have explained all this as effectively as Faline had done. I could now show off my knowledge to them, I smiled to myself.

"Never forget, John," Faline said in a polite, but author-itative tone, "whenever you have knowledge that others lack, don't feel great, but be grateful. That's the only way to increase your knowledge and stay on God's path."

What a fascinating combination of beauty, brains and compassion Faline was!

"Going back to that couple you saw earlier. They're an example of how to use leverage to create an investment asset. Remember, an investment asset is that asset which puts money into your pocket. Your money should go into buying only investment assets and not liabilities in the form of accounting assets, which are disguised as investment assets. This rule becomes even more important when you're using leverage, because leverage is nothing but multiplication. If you use investment assets, it will multiply, providing you with lifelong income. If you use leverage to buy liabilities disguised as accounting assets, then only your liabilities will multiply to give you lifelong costs in the form of maintenance and other running expenses. Therefore, leverage or debt should be used to buy only, I repeat, only investment assets."

Her words stung me. How foolish of me to buy luxury furniture for my house instead of the latest medical equipment; to take expensive overseas holidays, instead of paying to attend a medical seminar.

As I pondered over the common financial mistakes I had made at the time of saving and spending, of not taking proper financial insurance, of not unleashing the power of positive leverage and instead, getting poorer through negative leverage, Faline disappeared into a room indoors. It was a corner room that I had never been shown or encouraged to go to.

I sat on the sofa sipping another cup of chrysanthemum tea and enjoying the beauty and tranquility of this water town.

Once I was done with my tea, my curiosity got the better of me and I pushed open the door of the room that Faline had entered. I peeked in and my jaw dropped. Faline was sitting on a chair with an open notebook, a pen held loosely in her hand. The pen was moving on its own! I just stood there transfixed, too scared to move.

After some time, she stopped writing, or rather the pen stopped scribbling on the paper. She then turned toward the door and signaled me to enter. Still reeling from what I had witnessed, I followed her orders like a zombie, entering her room slowly. It was a very quiet room. Its walls and ceiling were painted white. There was just a wooden table, four wooden chairs in the middle of the room, along with a three-seater sofa. I sensed an unusual tranquility in the room. She told me to sip some of the prayer water and I did.

She made me sit beside her and when she looked at me, it felt as though a beam of light shot from her eyes into mine. She asked me to count from one to ten, and then say my name three times slowly.

"This will relax you as I try to link up with spirits."

She then said a brief prayer for the best and highest guidance from the greatest light. Once the preparatory formalities were over, she was ready to act as a psychic, as well as a medium.

Faline told me that although she had created links with spirits, she had a split link, meaning she could connected with more than one spirit. She told me that everyone in the spirit world spoke all at once, so she had to focus on the strongest link, that of a gentleman who had died from a respiratory problem. I immediately recognized the spirit as that of my father.

Faline continued, "he died from lung cancer, but he also had a weak heart. This man died in his 60s."

My father died at 64. I whispered, "Faline, he's my father, James Pinto."

She also told me he had suffered from a number of health problems before his death, and this was true. My father had been in and out of hospital so often in the years before his death that it had become like a second home to him.

Faline also told me he was a smoker, which again was true. Even after losing half a lung to cancer and undergoing bypass surgery, he wouldn't stop smoking. Faline informed me that my father was asking about his zip-up jacket. I knew exactly what he was talking about as it was the winter coat I had worn the day before I met Vijay.

Suddenly, another spirit interrupted the conversation. Faline mentioned a man in police uniform. I recognized it instantly as that of my uncle. He was a much-decorated hero of the Mumbai police. Faline said he was showing her his boots, helmets, rifles, bullets, shells and uniforms.

He also told her how he and my father loved to fish. Both our families used to drive down to the beaches of Gorai and Madh Island to park our campers, sleep right there on the beach and fish until we couldn't find any more in the Arabian Sea. By its shores, we would make campfires, cook the fish we had caught and eat our meals.

Next came my paternal grandmother, Marie Pinto. She and I were very close. Faline told me about my grandmother, who without any formal education had learned her life lessons at the School of Hard Knocks. She may have lacked textbook knowledge, but she was very familiar with money and its peculiarities. She worked very hard at keeping her family together, despite her husband leaving her with six children. She told Faline that she would give and give, doing whatever needed to be done to help her kids. My grandmother was not coming through in a pity-party manner, but just detailing the reality of her situation so that Faline could comprehend and articulate it.

My father came through again to say I was a workaholic, loved my studies and work, but never understood money and its rules. He complained about how I always believed in being a slave to money. I worked only for earned income and never strived to achieve passive or portfolio income. My grandmother's grouse was that I was ignorant of the strength of positive leverage, for I never understood how to use debt to increase my wealth.

I was mortified that even my ancestors were ridiculing my lack of knowledge about money.

My father held up a thermometer to Faline, calling it a stress-o-meter. He told her my stress level was currently sky high because of my financial, emotional and mental problems arising from my lack of financial knowledge.

Faline opened her eyes slowly and explained that she was trying to help people know that their dead loved ones were doing well and ready to communicate when the need arose.

"I am not only a medium but also a psychic. I will highlight certain soul characteristics of yours so you can improve and lead a fuller life.

Soul characteristics aren't just about our relationships in this life. We also have soul contracts from other lives that continue to affect us, both positively and negatively. So you might have soul contracts from a past life that are blocking you from something you've been trying to accomplish in this lifetime – such as a healthy relationship, career or financial success, health or fitness goals, or even creative fulfillment.

Integrity is important to you. So when you make a commitment, you'll sacrifice yourself to uphold it, even if it's a commitment from another life. As a result, over many lives, you have a lot of contracts that you are still committed to that are holding you back.

You have vowed to suffer. This prevents anything from coming easily to you. This must be removed."

She then told me to be prepared for my future mission.

"People will soon be coming to you with their physical, mental and financial challenges. You will provide them with the tools and resources to enable them to help themselves. It's not a question of whether you will do this, but rather, how you will meet everyone's needs."

It was, perhaps, for this reason that my friend had sent me on this journey across the world to learn the financial wisdom of the commandments.

Faline then revealed how my father's spirit had communicated with Vijay through his subconscious mind and encouraged him to educate me.

Once my reading was over, she went into a detailed explanation of how all human beings were spirits. A spirit means a soul together with its subconscious mind, which arrives on earth to take a physical form to learn, repay its karma and fulfill its spiritual mission. A human being is, therefore, made up of the soul, the subconscious mind, the physical body and the physical mind. The physical mind and body stay here and are destroyed after death, while the soul and subconscious mind are eternal and return to the spirit world. Heaven and Hell, she said, referred to different realms or planes in the spirit world. The purpose of the birth of every soul is an individual's spiritual progress, selfless help to other souls and the completion of his mission on earth. I learned from her that it was my spiritual mission to educate people about the financial commandments and their wisdom with the ultimate objective of elevating their lives, financially and otherwise.

She further informed me that good souls from heaven help earth souls from the spirit world. However, if a person is repaying his karmic debt, then the spirit souls will not be able to take away that person's problems, because he has to pay for his sins; however, they will certainly heal and give courage to see them through the difficult times. She clarified that since I was on the wrong path to suicide, the soul of my father had, through the subconscious mind of Vijay Desai, requested him to put me on the right financial path, so that

I could then fulfill my earthly mission of educating others about money.

After lunch that day, as I relaxed on the sofa, I went over all that I had experienced during the past few days. I had never imagined when I boarded the flight from Kabul for Shanghai, that I would learn the eternal truths of life over here, especially from a 25-year-old woman. I also understood the mysterious functioning of the spirit world and about life after death. I realized that financial wisdom was not just about money and how to get rich, it was a permanent medicine for elevating one's soul to the highest level.

"Talking to spirits is also a form of leverage," Faline said as I sipped my afternoon chrysanthemum tea. "In a few minutes you can acquire the wisdom of many births and know your true purpose in life. This is the power of multiplication and positive leverage." I nodded as I polished off a plate of Chinese snacks of *douhua* and *yutougao*.

That evening we moved around Zhujiajiao town and visited the market. Faline also took me to some of the town's great bridges, including the Fangsheng Bridge. She said no visit to Zhujiajiao could be complete without seeing the bridges, most of which were built during the Ming and Qing dynasties (1344–1911). The old town is fully connected by 36 bridges of different styles – from wooden to stone to marble. The town's ancient streets are lined with representative ancient buildings and gardens. The most noteworthy of them is the Ke Zhi Yuan manorial garden.

We turned into a street of carpet sellers and noticing my interest, Faline said, "buying a good carpet isn't easy. You, of course, need to know about knots, fiber and dye. But you also need to know how to bargain. In many ways, buying a good carpet at a bargain price is like getting a loan at the best possible rate of interest. I would love to instruct you on this."

I readily agreed and Faline helped me buy a very good carpet at an extremely attractive price, much to the consternation of the carpet sellers.

The cashier appeared to be more educated than his position suggested. Faline revealed that he was once the manager of the largest bank branch in Zhujiajiao. But even so, he had little knowledge of the rules of money, debt and leverage. He failed to recognize the dangerous effects of negative leverage. He took a huge bank loan using his influence as a manager, blew it all on costly overseas holidays, five-star dinners, etc., and also created bad capital assets like a beach house, expensive cars and luxury furniture. He had to eventually auction off his house to pay his debts. Not just that, his children's education was disrupted and his wife was forced to take up a job.

"So now, here he is, from a high-flying bank manager to a cashier in a carpet shop."

I was reminded of Duan telling me Warren Buffet's quote, "if you buy the things which you don't require, very soon you will have to sell the things that you require."

I got up early the next morning, but Faline had already left for Shanghai to help the parents of a small child, who was very sick despite the best efforts of the doctors.

I spent a quiet day, reflecting on my newly acquired knowledge.

Faline returned at 4 pm, looking as refreshed as ever and with the happy news that the child would be saved. Something from his previous life was interrupting his current life, but through regression therapy she had made the small child modify the *akashic* records.

Faline informed me that within an hour, I would be leaving for Shanghai airport to fly to Sydney, Australia. There I would meet an old man of 65 and his daughter of 40. She then went into her special room to return with a small envelope.

"The time has come for me to hand over what is meant for you," she said as she carefully gave me the envelope. It came with a small memento that carried a picture of a mathematical formula, $1 + 1 = 11$.

Faline smiled as I puzzled over it, as if trying to explain that this was all about leverage. When one portion of positive leverage is added to an existing portion of one's wealth, it would not just add up to two, but instead multiply one's wealth to 11. Without wasting any more time, I carefully opened the envelope.

The Money Multiplier

Just as a lion multiplies its chance of making a big kill while hunting in groups, so can you multiply your wealth by unleashing the power of positive leverage.

Never fear taking risks in life. Staying in one's comfort zone is the biggest risk of all, since it is the most dangerous and uncertain place on this planet. Leverage is simply the multiplication of your money wealth. Contrary to popular opinion, positive leverage is not risky if you know how to harness its power. However, lack of proper leverage might hinder your goal of achieving financial independence. Positive leverage is that debt which multiplies your money by putting money into your pocket, while negative leverage is that debt which reduces your money by taking money out of your pocket. Remember that every time you do what you fear, including taking positive leverage, you take back the power that fear has stolen from you and reclaim the powerful strength lying within you. Whether dealing with humans or money, eyes can be deceptive. Learn to recognize the difference between an investment asset and a liability disguised as an accounting asset. Never use leverage to buy a liability disguised as an accounting asset, because it will not only take money out of your pocket in the form of maintenance and running expenses, but also in the form of interest payments on your debts. Be it an individual, corporation or government, a debt trap is difficult to escape from. Remember, greed is your biggest enemy while leveraging. For ultimate power of positive leverage, you must aim to reach the stage of net positive cash flow. Once you have reached this stage, you start making money for nothing. You should never leverage for portfolio income (capital gains), but only for passive income (regular income in the form of rent, dividend, interest, etc). Along with positive leverage, inflation is your partner, because inflation is what makes you borrow costlier money today to pay back your loan in the future in cheaper money. Properly harnessing the power of positive leverage will allow you to be your own bank, multiplying your wealth by using the money multiplier factor and thereby, creating your own investments out of thin air. You can reduce uncertainty while dealing with life, money or debt by improving the most important leverage of all – your own financial knowledge and wisdom.

Where Did My Pie Go?

It was with a very heavy heart that I waited at Shanghai airport after wishing my spiritual and money mentor, Faline Cheong, adieu. She was a teacher who had no certifications, but whose lessons were for keeps.

My flight was right on time. Once inside the aircraft, I got to indulge in another round of Chinese delicacies. My mind kept going back to what I had learned from Faline. It was so easy to communicate with her. I did not have to utter a single word. All I had to do was think about something and she would immediately read it. And what financial wisdom she had shared with me! I learned not to worry about taking risks in life, realizing that being in one's comfort zone is the biggest risk of all as it is the most dangerous and uncertain place on this planet. She helped clear my foggy thoughts by showing me that positive leverage was the most powerful mathematical tool in the financial world, one that multiplied my money and my wealth. And when I unleashed the power of positive leverage, I got money for nothing. It was the license to print my own money.

I don't know when I fell asleep, but when I woke up it was 5.30 am. Subconsciously, I had remembered not to rob time from my own life, even while traveling in an aircraft. I felt very fresh, relaxed and enlightened. Maybe I had encountered the astral soul of Faline in my sleep. I was really enjoying this journey. After a refreshing cup of tea and breakfast, I was ready for my new destination.

On landing at Sydney airport, the first thing I noticed was the time. It was 8.10 am. This was the seventh day of my incredible soul-searching, financial journey. As I stood outside Sydney airport waiting for my new teacher, a lady came up to me and wished me.

"Good morning, Mr Pinto," she smiled. "I am Adaline Jones, the living embodiment of the fifth financial commandment."

On wishing her a good morning, I noticed her gorgeous smile. Adaline told me that she was in her mid-40s, but she looked at least ten years younger. She was wearing a black dress adorned with beads and covered in stripes. Her skin was flawless and her teeth, almost perfect. She was enthusiastic and extremely self-confident. She had decorated her blonde hair with a beautiful white flower that contrasted nicely with her black dress.

"That way, sir," she said, pointing toward a small, but well-maintained car. "We will be going to my hometown, Kiama, which is about 90 miles from Sydney."

"Kiama? I have never heard of this place," I blurted.

Adaline remained unperturbed by this rude remark. "It is famous for its spectacular coastline and pastoral scenery. Dairy farming and quarrying are the most important activities here. Its economy's mainstay is agriculture and now, tourism," Adaline said politely.

This was my first encounter with an Australian and I was very impressed by the graciousness of my new acquaintance.

Half an hour after we set off, the car turned into a rough dirt road that seemed to follow a small valley. We bounced down it some way, flanked by thick forests and passed under a wooden arch. Finally, we pulled up in an open space.

She lived in a renovated, brick veneer home, perched on the edge of the ocean with a stunning view of the bay, rocky headland and beach. We were greeted by an old man with a wrinkled face, supporting himself on a bamboo stick.

"Hey, Good Morning, John" he said slowly. "I am Christopher Jones, Adaline's father. I live here in *her* beautiful house. Welcome to Kiama!"

Christopher looked to be in his mid-60s. I was immediately drawn to his eyes. To gaze into them was to drown in a pool of tranquility and wisdom. Adaline rescued me from their magnetic pull by inviting me to look around the house.

I marveled at the modern furnishings: the floorboards throughout the property, the tall windows that let in plenty of natural light and the two huge timber decks flowing directly from the large living rooms. The house included a fully equipped kitchen that overlooked the outdoor deck and entertainment area, the two living rooms and a fenced yard for the kids. The many touches of luxury on the property included a bathroom outfitted with a spa, the sparkling floorboards, a spacious balcony, new carpets in the two bedrooms and fresh paint on the walls and exterior. I also noticed a single garage outside and a reasonably level backyard. Deeper into the yard were a number of farm animals: cattle, sheep, goats, chicken, pigs and even a few horses.

Adaline told me that she was into cattle rearing, livestock farming and a poultry business. She took me to where the animals were. I was surprised at how she had organized the place, every animal had its own little quarters. The food, too, was arranged so that every animal got its due share. None of the larger animals could bully the smaller, weaker ones. I also noticed that the farm hands paid equal attention to all animals, large and small.

As my admiration for Adaline grew, I couldn't wait to see what she would have to teach me about finance and money.

"Why have you gone to such lengths to ensure every animal has its own place," I wondered aloud.

"Just as every human desires his own space, animals, too, need their own space. I've ensured that every creature, large like a horse or small like a chicken, has its own proper place. The food is also divided properly in the proportions that each one of them requires and deserves. This is called asset allocation."

I was hearing this term for the first time. As I looked quizzically at Adaline, she continued, "this is the most important tenet of money education. It simply means giving the right importance to each variable, whether in life or while dealing with money and investments."

"I understand that in the context of life, but how does it apply to money and finance?"

"Look, John," she said. "Do you put all your eggs in one basket?"

"Yes," I replied without thinking.

"Has it ever happened that the basket slipped from your hand and all the eggs broke?"

"Oh, yes. Many times".

"So what did you learn from it, John?"

"That I have to be more careful with the basket the next time?"

Adaline smiled broadly. "That may be one of the solutions, but not necessarily the best one. Have you ever thought that if you had distributed your eggs in, say, five different baskets, you would have lost only 20% of your eggs if any one of the baskets had slipped. The remaining 80% of your eggs in the other baskets would have been completely safe. The same goes for your money and investments."

This was so basic and yet I had never thought of it that way!

"If you keep all your money in a single bank and for whatever reasons that bank goes bankrupt, you'll lose all of your hard-earned savings. However, if you were to segregate and apportion that money to five different banks, then you would lose only 20% of your money if one of those banks were to become bankrupt."

Excellent idea. I vouched to do just that as soon as I was back in India.

"The same goes for your investments, John," Adaline explained. "When you invest all your funds in a single asset class, then you run the risk of financial loss, money loss, purchasing power loss and income loss."

Now, I was a bit lost. What did all these terms mean?

"All my money is in safe bank deposits and earns a guaranteed interest income," I said. "Where is the question of incurring all these losses you just mentioned?"

"But are you always able to buy what you thought you could with the interest income on your bank deposits?"

I thought for a bit and then said, "no, many times I have had to cut back on my plans, although I made a careful calculation of how much interest I would receive at the time of making the deposit, comparing it against the cost of what I wanted to buy. But invariably, my interest income would somehow fall short of the desired money on maturity, as if somebody was stealing money from my account."

"Yes John, there was somebody stealing money from your account." On seeing me shocked, Adaline hastened to add, "it was the monster of inflation. It eats into your savings and reduces its purchasing power."

"So what is the solution to this problem of inflation?"

"You have to pick those investment options which benefit from inflation, such as commodities and equity stocks."

Our conversation was abruptly interrupted by Adaline's father, Christopher, who called us in for lunch.

As I walked toward Christopher, who was waiting at the front door, I noticed he was wearing a shiny-looking sweater, worn-out jeans and a pair of cheap slippers. He appeared to be unhappy like he was punishing himself for something.

"Come on, John," he said in a booming voice. "The food is ready to be served."

The dining hall was small, but elegant. In the center stood a wooden dining table and four chairs. A thoughtfully placed flower pot on the table added just the right touch of color to the ambience. At the far end was a wall unit with glass doors.

Christopher offered me some beer, which I greedily grabbed, having missed it dearly for the past seven days. As Christopher and I drank, Adaline sat beside us quietly and had her soup. Soon, the food was served. "Beef with yoghurt and a perfect dish to go with chilled beer," Chrisopher said.

When we had downed our second beer, Adaline stepped in and said, "that's it, gentlemen. The limit for beer has been reached. It's now time to allocate your limited resource, your stomach, to other options."

Saying this, she directed us to dishes of pepper-crusted lamb with plum chutney, lemon chicken in outback and the coat of arms.

"These scrumptious coat of arms are an Australian delicacy made of kangaroo and emu meat," Christopher explained.

As I explored the typical Australian spread, I wondered what Adaline had meant by referring to the stomach as a limited resource.

Dessert was just a single portion of sticky date pudding and Boysenberry cheesecake, but boy, was it heavenly!

"I hope the allocation toward the beer, appetizers, main course and dessert was appropriate," Adaline asked out of the blue. I found it odd, but thought perhaps this was the Australian way to ask guests if they had enjoyed a meal. She suggested I take a short rest before heading out to the beach that evening.

The room I was alloted was small. Its floor was covered in tiny, light brown marble tiles and its walls were painted in soothing colors. The comfortable-looking bed was very inviting, but I decided to shower before taking a nap.

The luxurious bathroom's wooden walls were lined with a hand shower, a head shower and four small massage showers. In one corner was a rectangular bath tub, its walls rising about two feet above the floor. The bathroom felt warm and humid. As I stepped into the bathtub, some of the water spilled, reminding me of how Archimedes discovered the law of buoyancy. I thought maybe I would have my own eureka moment and discover the meaning of that mystery word, *allocation*.

I must have slept for at least a couple of hours before I was woken up to join the family for evening tea and snacks. As I indulged in a hot cup of organic chamomile tea with macadamia bread, apricot jam, anzacs followed by meat pie and sausage rolls, Adaline said, "notice the proper allocation between chamomile tea, which relaxes, relieves pain and is good for digestion, besides being loaded with vitamins and minerals, and the macadamia bread and apricot jam, which has the right mix of complex carbohydrates and sugar. The meat pie and sausage roll are good sources of protein and essential fatty acids. This is a complete meal, giving you all the essential nutrients in the right proportions."

What I was learning was fantastic, but the mystery of allocation still continued.

After a few more minutes, we headed to the beach right behind her house. The short main street, only a few meters from the beach, was crammed with small eateries, bars, nightclubs, travel agents and internet cafes. A looped road ran on the flat land below the hills. Most of the development appeared to have taken place in the area between this and the main street, with the hillsides offering views of the resorts and other residences.

"Most of Australia's population lives close to the coastline and the beach has long occupied a special place in the Australian identity. The Australian coastline is where three of the world's great oceans (Pacific, Indian and Southern) meet. For many Australians, the beach is a place of work. Early occupations for people in coastal communities included pearling, oyster farming, whaling, sealing, and fishing," Adaline elaborated.

The beach was beautiful and the waters of the Indian Ocean were crystal clear, unlike in India.

"Look there, John," she said pointing toward a mother and her four children. "See how she has properly distributed the ice cream and candies between her four children. This is perfect allocation."

There was that word again, 'allocation'.

Suddenly, I noticed her father's eyes clouding. After a brief silence, he said, "whether i's investments or children, it's not possible to know who will turn out to be good in the future. So instead of speculating about the winner, it's better to allocate resources properly among all of them."

It was becoming clearer to me that allocation meant the proper apportioning of the various options at ones disposal. But now I wanted to get to the bottom of this father-daughter relationship. I was sure something was amiss.

After spending a great evening together, we returned home for supper. First to arrive at the table was Sydney salad, lettuce mixed with melon and plenty of mayonnaise. Then came the appetizers, gumleaf (scented smoked salmon), bruschetta and crab avocado cups.

As I enjoyed my super supper, Christopher broke the silence, "I know, John, that you are curious about my relationship with my daughter. So listen carefully. Here it is and a shameful one at that."

I almost let my imagination run wild before Christopher poured his heart out to me.

"I had three daughters. My wife died when they were very young. She was a most loving wife and mother and her death left me shattered. But I knew I had to soldier on, at least for the sake of the girls. So I put my heart and soul into my work to make money and build my business empire. I soon made a fortune. Around the same time, I became very attached to my oldest daughter, Charlotte, and spoiled her silly, neglecting my two other daughters, Adaline and Gabriella.

Over the years, as my name, wealth and fame increased, so did my partiality toward Charlotte." Overcome with emotion, he paused and took a big gulp of water before continuing.

"My affection for my oldest daughter reached such a level that I gave her all my wealth – my assets, factories, businesses and investments – everything. But in return, I was betrayed. She and her husband took all my wealth and threw me out of the house. I was reduced to a pauper. She then sold all my assets and businesses and settled down in some European country. I have no clue as to her whereabouts. Meanwhile, my youngest daughter Gabriella, unable to bear the pain of being separated from me, died from brain hemorrhage."

At this point he broke down and Adaline put a comforting hand on him. Gathering himself, Christopher said, "it was this daughter who took me in when I was out on the streets and she has taken care of me ever since. She rescued me from the street when I had left her on the street to die. I owe my life to her. It was a curse to have a daughter like Charlotte, but it's a blessing to have a daughter like Adaline. She has lived up to her name, Adaline, which means 'noble'.

You know, John, the problem with my approach was improper allocation of both my money and my love. I gave all my money and love to only one daughter and I lost both."

What a paradoxical statement, I thought. Then I remembered a close friend who had borrowed some money, promising to pay it back, but then disappeared without a trace.

"So, you see, John," started Adaline, "allocation is the most important thing in this world and affects all facets of our life, personal or professional. Allocation, simply put, means maintaining a proper balance. There has to be balance between work and play, saving and spending and in the love for our loved ones. Even nature observes balance, as can be seen from night and day or the different seasons. Life without balance leads to disaster. Similarly, in the world of money and investment, the most important principle is balance or allocation. It is the basis of all the financial commandments. With proper asset allocation, 90% of your money and investment woes will be solved. On the other hand, if you don't do a proper asset allocation, you can hardly hope to achieve financial independence."

Later that evening, as we enjoyed more Australian delicacies, such as beef with prunes and kangaroo meat fillets, topped off with a traditional dessert, pavlova, what struck me was the quiet devotion and love of a daughter for her father. I also remembered to make space for each category of food brought to the table that night to ensure I had a balanced meal. Again, I didn't stay up late, remembering to allocate adequate time for sleep, so that I felt well-rested the next day.

I was up with the sun the next morning. After breakfast, Adaline and I headed to the market. I watched with fascination as she went about picking her fruits, vegetables, meat, fish, groceries, making sure she allocated her spending money in such a way that all items were covered.

"Although these are small expenses, John," she explained, "the way we do the small things determines the way we will do the bigger ones. If we don't form and practice good habits then we automatically sow the seeds of bad habits."

As I thought about Adaline's life, I couldn't help pointing out one mistake she had made in setting out her life's priorities. While struggling to make a respectable life and take care of her father, she had not allocated time for her own marriage.

This meant a certain imbalance in her life. When I voiced my thoughts, she accepted it very graciously.

Over tea that afternoon, Adaline told me that by investing all my funds in bank fixed deposits I had not only surrendered the purchasing power of my money to inflation, but actually made my portfolio more risky.

I didn't get it at first. How could fixed deposits in a bank be riskier than equity?

"An all-debt portfolio is not the least risky portfolio. In fact, adding a small amount of stock to an all-debt portfolio can actually reduce the risk slightly while improving the return considerably," she clarified.

"I should teach this to my doctor friends who are wary of equity investments."

"The corollary to the above would be that the addition of a small amount of bond to an all-stock portfolio would significantly reduce risk, while only marginally bringing down the return."

This was for all the stockaholics, the ones who invest only in stocks for growth, forgetting the inherent risks involved in such a strategy.

"Generally speaking, mid- and small-cap stocks are more risky than large-cap ones. Therefore, small-cap stocks might need more dilution from bonds than large-cap ones."

Yes, that was something I needed to teach my young nurse who invested her entire salary in risky mid-cap stocks.

I retired to my room after lunch and spent a long time pondering over my incredible journey. It was almost a week since I had left home, but I had lost any real sense of time. My anxiety about my work and the financial mess I was in had come down considerably. It was, perhaps, the financial wisdom that I was constantly receiving, living and experiencing that was raising my morale to a level I had never imagined.

Later, Adaline told me she had organized a big dinner party for me that evening, and had invited all her neighbors and friends. I was really touched by this gesture. After all, I was a complete stranger to her.

That evening Adaline's house was one crowded and noisy place. The sound of music filled the rooms and children made merry, as copious amounts of food and drinks were passed around. Seeing the children play with the barn animals reminded me of my own daughter when she was young. I suddenly longed to see my family and right away sat down to compose a sweet message and send it to them.

"Meet Mr Dominick Williams. He works in equity sales in one of the large brokerage firms in Sydney," Adaline interrupted, leading a young man to me.

"Oh! I work for a brokerage house only because I had to sell my own firm," Dominick volunteered before disappearing into the woods. Catching my dazed look, Adaline explained, "he was once the owner of one of the reputed mid-sized brokerage firms that he inherited from his father. However, instead of concentrating on building his clientele, he was more interested in personal equity investments and speculation, and paid no attention to proper asset allocation. The last bear market in equities wiped him out. He not only lost his brokerage firm, but also a chance of earning good returns in the commodities bull market that accompanied the equity bear market."

"But you just said he lost money in an equity bear market. Where did this commodity bull market come from? I suppose all asset classes must simultaneously see a bear market, right?"

"No John. All assets move in business and economic cycles of their own and while one asset is in a bear market there might, simultaneously, be another asset class in a big bull market of its own."

As I meditated on this, Adaline introduced one Mrs. Emily Boon.

"She runs a lottery ticket stall in the market."

"I would have been running a big supermarket if I had not blown it all up."

Again, clearing the confusion, Adaline said, "Mrs. Boon won $1,000,000 in a lottery. She borrowed against that money, creating negative leverage and then invested the entire amount in a beach house, hoping to flip it at a higher price. The real estate market collapsed and so did her dream of flipping it. Her house was foreclosed and she had to sell a number of her good investments to settle the bank mortgage. Here was a combination of negative leverage and lack of asset allocation – a violation of two important financial commandments." I immediately remembered Faline lessons on negative leverage.

That night I remained very quiet after the noisy party and went over all the avoidable money mistakes that so many people make. If only they, too, could partake of the financial wisdom that I was receiving so generously.

The next morning was also quiet. As I watched Adaline go about her morning chores, she said, "work toward, achieving financial independence by ensuring proper allocation of the right income-earning investment assets. Almost 90% of portfolio variability is due to asset allocation, while only 10% of the variability in portfolio performance is due to market timing and stock selection. The only thing in your control is asset allocation and the good news, as I just mentioned, is that 90% of portfolio variability is due to asset allocation.

The broader asset groups of equities, bonds, commodities and real estate, besides art and currencies, will lead you to the gateway of long-term wealth creation and sustenance. Portfolios behave differently from their individual constituents. The aim of optimal asset allocation is not to invest only in safe assets, but to invest in a combination of safe and risky assets. Their combined risk is much less than that of the individual constituents and which, at the same time, offer higher returns. Therefore, focus on the behavior of your portfolio and not its constituents. Small portions of your portfolio will often sustain serious losses, but will cause only minor damage to the whole portfolio.

Learn how much risk you can tolerate, both financially and emotionally. For example, if emotionally you can't see your investments depreciate by 50% over the short-term, then equities probably might not be the right thing for you. But by removing equity from your portfolio, you are removing one of the greatest wealth creators over the long-term and income that will give you tax-free returns irrespective of your tax status."

Yes, this was probably the biggest mistake in most people's portfolio allocation - not enough earmarked for equities.

But Adaline was not done. "There may not be any real need for you to venture into purchasing stocks or bonds on your own if your knowledge, time, resources or money don't permit it. An investor can very well earn almost similar returns by purchasing them through a mutual fund or similar route. The key to long-term wealth creation is to build a correct portfolio of assets. The individual stocks and bonds will lose their individuality in it.

Finally, don't forget one thing, John," she summed up, "whether it is life or investments, change is the only constant thing in this world. So keep periodically rebalancing, reviewing, changing and refining your portfolio allocation in line with your financial goals."

Then, with a smile, she said, "I know this is a lot to absorb all at once. So this is the best time to give you what you have traveled so far for." Opening her handbag, she carefully removed an envelope and extended it toward me.

I noticed a small memento with the envelope. It contained the picture of a lioness giving milk to her four cubs in equal proportion. I smiled and slowly opened the envelope.

Correct Allocation Matters the Most

While managing your assets, the only thing in your conscious control is asset allocation, which is in fact responsible for 90% of portfolio variability.

Be in no hurry to change your finances overnight as you will not be ready to bear the consequences both mentally and physically. Patience is required as wealth needs to be built gradually, dollar by dollar. Sustenance and long-term wealth accumulation is a boring, mechanical process called asset allocation. Just as we dread monotony in routine, your money dreads the monotony of the allocation of its assets. Respect your money and it will honor you in return by staying and growing with you. If you are in control of your asset allocation, your money will be kind enough to control 90% of your portfolio variability. The broader asset groups of equities, bonds, commodities, real estate, art and currencies will lead you to the gateway of long-term wealth creation and sustenance. All assets move in business and economic cycles of their own. While one asset might be in a bear market, there may, simultaneously, be another asset class in a big bull market of its own. Risk is a relative concept; what may be risky for one, might be a cakewalk for another. An all-bond portfolio is not the least risky portfolio. In fact, adding a small amount of stock to an all-bond portfolio actually reduces the risk slightly while improving the return considerably. The aim of optimal asset allocation is not to invest only in safe assets, but to invest in a combination of safe and risky assets whose combined risk is much lower than that of the individual constituents and, at the same time, offers higher returns. Therefore, focus on the behavior of your portfolio and not its constituents. Small portions of your portfolio will often sustain serious losses, but will cause only minor damage to the whole portfolio. Just as you have to constantly replenish and nourish your body, you must also periodically keep reviewing and refining your portfolio allocation with changing financial goals.

Budgeting for a Marathon

It was 9.30 am and a bright, sunny morning. I was waiting at Sydney airport for my flight to Nairobi, Kenya. I had read Nairobi was also known as the 'green city in the sun'. It was my first visit to Africa. I knew I had a long flight of around 15 hours ahead of me. Nairobi was approximately seven hours behind Sydney. Mulling over this time difference, I suddenly wished I could rewind my life and live it armed with my newly acquired financial knowledge, thanks to the generosity of my dear friend, Vijay.

After a quick lunch in the plane, I settled down for a long rest. I went over all my recent experiences and lessons, and thought a lot about my family. How I wished that instead of working for money, I had made my money work for me. I would have had so much more time to spend with my family; I could have gone to all my son's football games; I could have been there at my daughter's first elocution contest; I could have been there for my wife when she was young and craved my attention; I could have taken care of my father when he was old and in the hospital. I vowed that once back home, I would make my newfound financial wisdom a way of life.

With that promise to my soul, I fell into deep sleep. The journey was long and tiring. I spent my time sleeping, eating and thinking about the financial wisdoms. Finally, the plane had reached its destination and I was refreshed and ready for the next adventure.

As I stood outside the Nairobi airport, I noticed it was around six in the evening. The sun was just about to disappear below the horizon and a full moon promised to bathe the city in its soft light.

"Hey John, this is Richard Omondi, your teacher in the long-distance race called life."

In front of me stood a tall, athletic black man. He had shiny black hair, gray eyes and dark skin, like the color of roasted pecans. I was immediately drawn to his warm personality.

"I hope your journey was comfortable and you are feeling well-rested, because we are going to take an evening walk to my house." Saying this, he picked up my luggage, leaving just a small carry bag for me. We walked a bit and at the end of the road, he pointed toward what looked like an intra-city highway. "That way, John. My house is just five miles from here."

"What?" I cried. "Five miles?"

Richard remained unperturbed, "yes, just five miles."

For the first time that evening, I began to feel the anxiety rising within me. Who was this guy? The 15-hour journey left me jet-lagged and now he expected me to walk five miles to his house? Was this the way to behave with guests?

Then I reminded myself that Vijay had done right by me all long. Why should I doubt his judgment now? I calmed myself down and tried to keep pace with my new acquaintance.

I was too tired to notice much of Nairobi's streets, although, they did seem rather chaotic. Pedestrians ruled the roads and the few cars that I did see seemed to work around them. To me, it looked like nothing short of a miracle that there were no collisions.

The tiny cars, the many billboards, the homes and shops fashioned out of corrugated metal and the humid air reminded me of my home, Mumbai. While I dragged my feet behind me, Richard kept up at a brisk pace, unmindful of the weight he was carrying.

It was a while before we arrived at the majestic home of Richard Omondi, with its high walls, soaring ceilings and wide corridors. The garden was covered in rows of colorful flowers with labels and decorated with intricately carved stone statues etched with what I supposed were ancient African characters. On the walls hung garlands of fresh roses, which gave off a fragrance that instantly lifted my spirits. Also on display were medals and cups of various sizes with the names of the races and competitions they represented beautifully embossed on them.

"There is your room," Richard said pointing to a large door opening out from the living room. "Freshen up quickly as dinner is ready to be served."

I sure was looking forward to a good meal. As I changed into a fresh set of clothes, I could hear the sound of children playing. I saw a boy of around eight years old and a girl of around five.

"Meet my son, Elvis, and my daughter, Belinda," said the sweet voice of a lady of around 30. "I am Sarah, Richard's wife." She was beautiful and looked incredibly fresh for this hour of the day.

"I see you have made your introductions," Richard said as he joined us.

I joined the family as we made our way through a long corridor to the dining room. The big table stood out in the spacious room. Each of its eight chairs was painted in a different color. How I wished my wife could have been with me. She loved colorful things and would have so enjoyed being in Richard's house. I felt a pang of guilt that I never had the money to take her on exotic holidays.

"Kenyan food typically is a combination of traditional African dishes, tribal delicacies, as well as Arabian and European delicacies. Rice, bread, chapati and vegetables are the staple foods. Potatoes are eaten in plenty here and are the main ingredient in most dishes. Rice and vegetables are eaten with beef, chicken or fish preparations."

"Here comes the food," Sarah said as the servant came in with melamine serving dishes. "This is the *mtuza wa samaki*, or baked fish in a curry base. And this is the *kuku nazazi*, chicken made with coconut milk. The *maharagwe* here is a vegetarian preparation of spicy red bean and coconut milk. I also asked that *pilau* rice with beef stew be prepared in your honor. This is a specialty usually reserved for festive occasions."

Sarah urged me to get started, "or my husband will feed you with just his words."

Looking at the spread on the table, I noticed that the portions served seemed just right, as though someone had done a careful estimate of how much each person would eat. I also saw both Richard and Sarah have a long argument with their servant over what appeared to be a petty sum of money.

Catching my look of surprise, Richard said, "budgeting is very important. We have to be careful with our money and budget for now, as well as for the future."

Extending what seemed to be a penny toward me, Sarah added, "every drop counts."

I couldn't help thinking they were carrying things a bit too far, but I was quickly distracted by the appearance of dessert, *maandazi,* or sweet donut and coconut and sweet potato pudding.

When the children reached for another piece of the donut, Richard stopped them saying sternly, "learn to delay your gratification. Keep some for tomorrow."

Turning to me, he said, "the main problem with human beings is that they want to eat everything today out of their present and future money, creating a budget deficit for themselves."

I had no clue what he was talking about. Anyway, it was soon time to retire and Richard wished me good night, telling me we would embark on a long, mysterious adventure the next morning.

I woke up to the sweet aroma of Kenyan chai. I realized I had not moved a bone all night.

"Come on, dude," Richard shouted. "Hurry up! Remember the adventure I promised you?" I dressed quickly and went into the dining hall where a breakfast of chapati, baked egg, oatmeal stout, bread with margarine and banana, had been laid out.

"I hope our strong tea has rid you of any fatigue you had. Although India and China are the largest producers of tea, Kenya is its largest exporter," he added proudly. "You must eat a reasonable quantity of complex carbohydrates as you start your day. This will provide you with steady energy throughout the day. All whole grains like wheat and oats have complex carbohydrates. But if you're going on a long adventure, then you should also consume some amount of simple carbohydrates like raw sugar or better still, the sugar found in fruits, as well as proteins of the kind found in eggs, fish and chicken."

Had I been sent to Kenya to be educated in financial management or diet and nutrition?

"Your body is God's gift to you and you must take care of it. It is the soul's dress for fulfilling its mission on earth. Similarly, money is a source of fulfillment of your dreams, but you must know how to take care of it and budget for yourself. If you don't know how to protect your money, it will never stay with you."

"Hey, John," Sarah's sweet voice interrupted our conversation. "Richard is as good with money matters as he is with diet and nutrition. I owe my well-kept figure to him. He helped me lose 25 pounds in three months."

Twenty-five pounds in three months? Was she kidding?

But I had to admit, I had never seen such a toned body on a mother of two. I really did need some advice from Richard on my health, too. Despite being a doctor, I had picked up a number of bad eating habits while chasing after money and becoming a slave to it.

Richard suddenly sprang out of his chair and with a decisive air declared that we were heading to the Great Rift Valley. It was an hour-and-a-half drive from Nairobi. Despite the early hour, the sun was blazing, making the surrounding villages, green hills, waters appear brighter, clearer, sharper and more vibrant.

Richard told me that the numerous high-altitude training camps in the Great Rift Valley and Central Kenya attracted many international athletes, yearning to share in a little of the training that builds Kenya's long-distance marathon runners.

"From its panoramic perch above Lake Naivasha, the Great Rift Valley Lodge offers a breathtaking view of the sweeping floor of the world's largest valley. Would you like to go there?"

I readily agreed not realizing the mystery behind it. We then drove to the parking lot at the base of the hill.

"So, let's begin."

I was confused. Begin what?

"It's just ten miles uphill to the summit and 7,000 feet above sea level."

I was flabbergasted. Getting to the top of the Great Right Valley suddenly didn't seem like such a good idea.

"You must be joking!" I said.

"Certainly not, John."

"But I can't do this climb. I have never done anything like this before."

"We do many things for the first time in our lives. Walking, talking, sitting for an exam, having sex, earning money, committing money mistakes and then making that a habit. Never be afraid of forming new, good habits, John."

Richard began climbing. The thought of being in that desolate place alone and spotting wild animals was enough to set me off huffing and puffing behind him.

The climb was no cakewalk, but in my rush to be done with the ordeal, I raced ahead and had soon outpaced Richard. I ended up suffering severe muscle cramps. I started breathing heavily, my heart was pounding, I was drenched in sweat and I was dying of thirst. My head reeled and I collapsed on the rocks.

I came to my senses soon after Richard sprinkled some water on my face.

"What happened, my friend?" he said hauling me to my feet. I was mortified, and could sense that he had found a teaching moment.

"Your mistake was that you tried to run too quickly without estimating the overall distance, the stamina and time required. You used all your reserve energy immediately without budgeting for the future.

Whether running the race of life or money, you have to save fuel for the future. If you use all your resources today, then what about tomorrow? So always budget for yourself and remember to create a positive budget."

Saying these prophetic words, he once again broke into a sprint. I joined him, but this time I remembered to monitor my speed and energy levels. It was only now that I noticed our surroundings – the occasional fieldworkers, the birds squawking as they swooped through the trees and the sounds of small animals scurrying through the bushes.

After covering about half the distance, we took a short rest, and then continued jogging at a steady pace, saving our energy and budgeting for the future.

When we finally reached the top of the Great Rift Valley, my shirt was clinging to my back and my pants were glued to my legs. But the view from there was truly worth the trouble.

"So, what did you learn from the experience of running fast and fainting?" Richard asked mysteriously.

"I must do proper budgeting," I replied without even fully comprehending the meaning of the term 'budgeting'.

"A budget is simply a planned allocation of available resources. There can be two types of budget, surplus and deficit, and the choice is entirely yours as to which to select. When income exceeds expenses, you have a surplus budget, while when expenses exceed income, you have a deficit budget.

A budget surplus is essentially an excess of income over spending, be it a government, corporation or individual, over a particular period of time. The important words to note here are 'excess of income over spending'. Therefore, a budget deficit doesn't necessarily mean living below your means. It simply means expanding your means so that your expenses fit into it, leaving you with a surplus."

He continued with his education, "a budget surplus should be a priority. It should be a compulsory expense that you have to incur for yourself the same way as you pay your taxes to the government, loan instalments to the bank, telephone and electricity bills or your children's school fees.

Remember, my friend, that earning money is only the first step to becoming wealthy. But that alone isn't enough, you must also understand how the principles of money work in this modern information and currency age, and budgeting is an integral part of it."

Richard concluded his mini-lesson by saying, "budgeting is nothing but paying your own self."

Standing there at 7,000 feet above sea level, I was not sure what was more beautiful, the striking view or the wisdom I had just received from Richard. Whatever it was, I understood one thing, and that was to pay myself via a budget surplus.

Once back in Richard's splendid house after that long climb, I asked if the secret to his obvious success with money was saving and budgeting.

"I think you misunderstood me, John," came the worried reply. "By creating a budget surplus and paying yourself first, I didn't mean that you should become a miser. You can make some money by being frugal, but can't accumulate wealth and become rich. Even if you're able to accumulate some wealth by being frugal, you cannot achieve financial independence by being a miser."

"The starting point for creating a positive budget is to earn more money by using the unique talents that God has endowed each and every one with," Sarah piped in. "Recognize your talent, harness it and then use it to achieve success in your life, including your finances." Then turning to Richard, she said, "darling, why don't we play the *Financial Freedom Game* created by our mentor, Vijay Desai, after lunch. That will clear many of John's doubts."

"An excellent idea, Sarah! Call the kids, too. They enjoy the game and every time we play, they learn something new from it."

An elaborate spread soon appeared on the table of *kachumbari* salad, *mtuzi wasamaki, nyama choma, githeri* served with *wali* and chapati. In my excitement to play the game, I started gobbling up my food, but the look in Richard's eyes stopped me and reminded me of budgeting.

"The most precious resource of people isn't their time, it's their energy. Manage it well."

After polishing off some superbly cooked *mahamri* for dessert, we were all set for the game.

"This is a board game that puts individuals in real life situations and at every point forces them to take certain financial decisions. The player will encounter certain choice points, wherein he will have to make a choice on a specific financial concept. For example, at the choice point of earning, he will have to make a choice of whether he wants to work for money or wants his money to work for him. There will be some inducement for him to take the wrong decision in the form of immediate benefits. If he makes the wrong choice, he will realize it later when he either loses heavily or doesn't get an opportunity to earn handsomely. There may be some other choice points like say protecting his money, wherein he has to actually pay money today for making the right choice.

So it will hurt him today to make the right choice, but that will help him protect his money tomorrow. However, if he decides to take the easy route today, then he will have to pay heavily tomorrow."

Taking over from Richard, his wife continued, "similarly, the player will have to make budgeting, saving, investing, spending and leveraging decisions, wherein every wrong decision will give him immediate benefit, while every right decision will not give him instant gain, but will help him earn more, or lose less, in future.

The player will also have to take various other everyday decisions, such as whether to invest more money on higher studies or in business; keep extra money for the future or buy a car; use the limited available funds for important house repairs or fund a costly foreign vacation; take a working capital loan to expand his business or to take a mortgage loan to buy a bigger luxury house; invest in shares or bonds or gold; take positive leverage and expand business or just stay small and content; create positive cash flow via leverage; opt for financial insurance, etc. The game will involve important financial decisions at all points of dealing with money. The game will also teach the rules of money. It is a highly intelligent game, wherein the player's decision at every point will ensure whether he achieves financial independence or keeps struggling with money throughout his life."

I cried foul saying, "I'm still not aware of many of the financial commandments. That's not fair, Richard."

"And neither is life, my friend. Vijay has deliberately designed this game for you half-way through your journey, so that you may apply what you have already learned. The objective is to make you think and anticipate. Your future learning will become easier and much more interesting."

I thought it best not to argue and, as the guest, got to roll the dice first. It showed four, so I moved four spaces on the board to the spot where I could either buy a high rental real estate or a beach resort. Since the player did not have sufficient funds, he had the option of borrowing from the bank. I went for the most marvelous beach resort with the bank's money by mortgaging my assets.

Richard looked at Sarah with a grin.

Next was his son's turn. He was faced with the option of either going for an overseas holiday or a bank fixed deposit in a high interest rate environment. The child, predictably, opted for the holiday. Then came Belinda's turn and she was faced with the choice of buying an oil well or a costly dress. She went for the dress, exulting in how exotic she would look in it.

Sarah's options were gold ornaments or a gold biscuit. She chose the latter, much to my surprise. Not many women I knew would have spurned gorgeous, designer gold ornaments.

But her choice was hardly as shocking as Richard's. He picked high dividend-yield stocks over the latest BMW.

"Carry on, my friend. This game is not going to last long," he said.

Sure enough, I was soon bankrupt. The bank loan instalments had reached such gigantic proportions that I could no longer pay them. And the bank refused to lend me any more money. The worst part was that I had accumulated assets – if I could even call them that – a beach house and an expensive car that were just guzzling cash month after month in the form of property tax, maintenance, gas bills and the driver's salary. I also incurred expenses on account of exotic overseas travels and expensive gift items. Further, inflation was constantly rising and eating into the purchasing power of my money. So, on one hand I had accumulated all these so-called assets, that were just eating into my pocket without providing me any income, while on the other, I had to service the bank loan.

When I looked at Richard's position I saw high dividend-yield stocks, rental real estate and high yielding bonds, all of which were giving him a regular income. He had also purchased gold certificates, which were appreciating faster than the rate of inflation. And yes, he did take the occasional overseas trip or buy that fancy car, but he always ensured that it was the income from his assets, such as rent, dividend or interest that paid for those expenses. This kept his assets constant and allowed them to grow with time.

"It is time to use the financial freedom calculator, my friend," Richard said. The calculator immediately showed that I was bankrupt. It was, in fact, a unique calculator that did not classify my beach house and jaguar car as investment assets, but as a liabilities disguised as assets.

While the calculator declared me bankrupt, it showed Richard had a very healthy balance sheet and that he had reached the stage of financial freedom. His investment assets were paying off the expenses on the bad capital assets and unnecessary revenue expenditure.

"John, the reason you lost this money game is simply because you, like most people, don't know how to delay gratification."

"But how does delaying gratification help in making money?"

"That's the key to achieving financial nirvana, which most people don't understand and appreciate. The primary reason for a lot of pain is that most people can't control the desire for instant gain. Remember, there can be no long-term ultimate gain without short-term initial pain.

With the initial roll of the dice, you had the option of either buying an income yielding rental property or a cash guzzling expensive beach resort. What did you achieve by buying the beach resort? You simply got into a bad capital asset that wouldn't provide you with any income, but would regularly dip into your pocket for paying property taxes, maintenance and utility bills and mortgage instalments. It started robbing you of your money from day one. Now, compare that with a rental property. It puts money into your pocket from day one, month after month, it's making you rich, it's making you financially independent. Most importantly, the cash that you generate from rent will go into paying your bank debt. And one day, the bank loan will be fully repaid and your cash producing real estate would become yours for life. You'll get the rent on it for life, free of the bank instalment. In effect, it will become money for free. You'll start printing your own money. And what's more, once you start getting free money each month in the form of rent, then you can go and buy your fancy beach house. The rent on your rental property will pay for all the criminal expenses arising out of your beach house. That is what I mean by delaying gratification. First build your investment asset and then enjoy the fruits of it."

Sarah added, "you have to strive to reach such a stage where the income from your investment asset pays for the expenses on your bad capital assets and for unnecessary revenue expenditure. That's when you attain financial independence."

"Once the after-tax income generated on the investment asset exceeds the after-tax cost of the debt, the income generated from the investment asset becomes yours for keeps and your return on investment becomes infinite. That's when you become an ultimate financial genius, generating infinite return on investment," Richard reiterated his point.

As I digested all this, Richard continued, "always remember to budget for yourself first. Most people budget for everybody, be it the government, bankers, spouses, children and even for those expensive cars, costly vacations, etc., but they fail to budget for themselves. They pay everybody, but fail to pay themselves. And that's one of the biggest psychological mistakes that makes one poor. I say psychological mistake, because it is the mental attitude that is at play here. Always budget for yourself first. The secret is to create as much investment asset as is necessary to generate income that can pay for liabilities. And always remember that budget is an expense just like income tax, mortgage instalment, medical bills, electricity bills, telephone bills, school fees, etc. Have you ever thought about not paying income tax to the government? No. Treat budgeting the same way, as an expense that you cannot dispense with."

At this point Sarah interjected sagely, "I don't encourage people to merely cut spending on all kinds of necessary expenses to become rich. Firstly, that will not lead you to riches. And even if you become rich, it will not allow you to stay rich, because for that you should know how to create investment assets, which give you income rather than just cut spending. If there is no investment income then whose and what spending will you cut?"

I suddenly felt the weight of all this knowledge bearing down on me and was truly glad when my hosts suggested I rest a bit after evening *chai* and snacks, before heading to a Nairobi icon, the Uhuru Garden.

Uhuru, Richard told me, means 'freedom' in Swahili. The park is located at the spot Nairobi was declared free from British rule at midnight, December 12, 1963. It comprises a beautiful artificial lake and an assembly ground. It is the perfect setting to relax one's mind, body and soul.

"Do you know how a modern city budgets for itself?" asked Richard. Without waiting for an answer, he continued, "by creating beautiful parks and gardens where people can come and enjoy the authentic beauty of nature in an otherwise artificial world."

I went to bed thinking about all that I had learned that day – investment assets paying for bad capital expenditure and unnecessary revenue expenditure, as well as budgeting for myself the same way I would for others, such as the government, bank, etc.

Although I slept for fewer hours that night, I woke up fresh and toasty the next morning. I realized that whether it was money or sleep, it was not quantity, but quality that mattered.

After a quick breakfast of the traditional *ugali* and chai, we took off to Nairobi National Park. Nairobi is unique in that it has a wildlife park on its doorstep. Indeed, the city abuts the Nairobi National Park on all but the southern perimeter, so it is possible to see a rhino in the foreground of a photograph of high-rise office buildings. Some of the wildlife is migratory and when vegetation and water appear outside the park, they move out into Maasail and through the unfenced southern boundary. The Athi River at the park's far end forms a delightful natural boundary to the park. It provides shady walks through a riverside forest well-populated with monkeys and birds, and in the river pools laze the hippos and crocodiles. Large populations of giraffe, wildebeest, eland and Thomson's gazelle dominate the plains, and the strutting secretary birds and powerful ostriches serve to offer attractive counter-points. Nairobi National Park's pride of lions are well-served by the park staff and so is the cheetah. More recently, the park has been designated a rhino sanctuary and more than 50 rhinos have been moved into the park from remote parts of the country that were rife with poaching . The scenery along the south-western boundary is simply magnificent. It is an area of steep valleys created by streams joining the Athi River. Hyraxes are aplenty on the rocks alongside the road and the sharp-sighted may even spot a klipspringer or mountain reed buck. The boundary road offers splendid views of the Kitengela plains, which is also the dispersal area for the park's ungulates. Within Nairobi National Park's 117 square kilometers, there are more than 80 species of mammals and more bird species than can be found in the whole of the British Isles.

As I enjoyed the beauty of this African country, I wondered what Richard's profession was. When I asked him, he kept mum and I saw his wife Sarah's eyes begin to cloud. I apologized immediately thinking I had inadvertently touched a raw nerve.

"No John, don't be sorry. It's nothing to do with you. It was my own mistake."

What mistake?

Richard and his family could not have seemed more perfect to me, but then he broke his story to me.

"I used to be a top long-distance runner, with many medals in national, continental and international events under my belt. I had money, women, the works, literally, the world at my feet."

Richard looked contrite as his wife gave his hand a gentle squeeze.

He continued, "this beautiful house is also a result of the extravagance of those days. But just as I was becoming giddy with all the good times, fate had something else in store for me. One day, I fell off my motorbike after a night of drinking and partying with those selfish women. I tore the powerful anterior and medial cruciate ligaments of my knee. Although I was able to run again after undergoing surgery, I could not take the pressure of competitive long-distance running. It was only a matter of time before my name, money and all my so-called friends and fans had deserted me. I lost the battle of my life. The only ones to stand by me were my wife and children.

It was then that I accidentally bumped into Vijay Desai. He was in Nairobi for a charity supporting former long-distance runners. He introduced me to the financial commandments, educated me on managing my finances and encouraged me to start a training school for needy children. He gave my life a new purpose and lifted me from the depths of despair.

Now I teach children not only how to build up stamina for long-distance running, but also educate them about how fast to run initially, as well as how well to manage, conserve, save and budget one's energy for the future. I teach them how to stay ahead and win the race of life and money."

"The problem with Richard was that when he was earning in millions, he was spending in tens of millions, not saving anything for the future, not budgeting for himself," Sarah added.

"Yes, I was living on borrowed money, earning tons, spending in tens of tons and thinking that I will always earn in hundreds of tons in the future to keep paying for my extravagant lifestyle. Had I not met Vijay, I would have been a pauper today."

We spent the whole day in the national park. There I observed how even animals don't eat everything they get. They, too, save for a rainy day. Before falling asleep that cool African night, I vowed to always budget for myself and pay my family first.

As usual, I was up early the next morning. This had now become a habit. After breakfast, Richard and I were off to the High Altitude Training Center in Iten.

"It's perched on a cliff of the Great Rift Valley at almost 7,000 feet above sea level and draws top athletes, including world and Olympic champions, for high-altitude performance training. The altitude here is just perfect, neither too high, nor too low."

I could hear the pounding feet of dozens of runners as they trained on the winding mud tracks running through the quiet countryside.

"You know, John, it's very easy to reach the number one spot, but incredibly difficult to remain there, because when you're at the top, it's so easy to stop doing the very things that took you to the top.

For example, children work so hard in school to clear their exams, but once they have done that, they think it's the end of their education. The same thing happened to me."

Then turning to me he asked, "do you know what kind of financial person you are?" Seeing my raised eyebrow, he added quickly, "the first kind is the reckless person who earns a lot of money, but unfortunately, has negative net worth. This is the kind of person who might have a fat salary, but also a huge house mortgage, a posh beach home and costly cars bought with high-interest bank loans, as well as imported furniture, jewelry and overseas holidays, financed with high-cost credit cards and personal loans. This kind of person never accumulates wealth. He doesn't understand the difference between an asset and a liability, and adds on liabilities thinking they are assets.

I was that kind of person – earning in millions and spending in tens of millions on liabilities for which I had no use and which I mistook to be assets," he said remorsefully.

"The second kind is the financially illiterate person. No doubt, he has more wealth than the first kind and a positive net worth, but the amount of sacrifice he has to make for that wealth is much more than what he gets in return. This is the kind of person who doesn't understand the basic principle of money. He earns a good income but puts it all in so-called safe instruments such as a bank fixed deposit. True, he gets a fixed guaranteed income, but that turns out to be a pittance after deducting tax and adjusting for inflation. He always works hard, saving more of the money he makes.

Then there is the third kind who invests his own money in productive assets such as equities, rental property or inflation hedges, such as gold and silver. This kind belongs to a clever category of investors who convert their income to wealth by basically converting their earned income into passive and portfolio income.

And finally, there is the fourth and the last category of persons who display the highest degree of financial literacy. This kind invests not only his own earned income in productive assets, but also borrows, leverages and invests the borrowed funds in productive assets. He understands the basic principles of how to use money to create money. He recognizes that cash flows from productive assets have to be good enough to repay the interest on his loan. In short, he unleashes the ultimate power of positive leverage."

I instantly remembered my lessons in positive leverage from a former teacher, Faline Cheong, the mind reader. And here was Richard, brushing up my knowledge at the great heights of the Great Rift Valley.

After lunch that day, I sat in my room reflecting on how Richard had lost everything - his career, money, family's respect and love and then, how he had stood up, fought back and today, was not only leading a perfect life himself, but had also elevated the lives of poor runners by training them in the art he knew best. He was a perfect example of the saying, 'you can't beat a person who won't give up'.

That evening, Richard and Sarah took me on a city excursion, which gave me the chance to take some great photographs and indulge in some hard bargaining. I got to see the stately Parliament buildings, Kenyatta International Conference Centre, and look at the Nairobi skyline from atop the KICC. We also visited the Kenya National Archives and Watatu Art Gallery, as well as the Snake Park and the National Museum.

I came back to Richard's home tired but happy and eager for a warm meal. Over dinner that night, Sarah taught me about compounding and its magical powers.

"The beauty of creating a budget surplus is that time becomes your friend, exposing you to the magical benefits of compounding.

You're a middle-aged doctor of 45, earning a good income. Now say you invest ₹2,00,000 per annum at 10% return. Your money will grow to ₹1.14 crore in 20 years, when you are 65. Your problem is that, now, time is not your best friend since you are already 45. But say someone, who has just started earning at 25, invests just ₹1,00,000 per annum for 35 years till he retires, he will have a corpus of ₹2.71 crore. A neat sum, right?"

This was incredible. Even someone from a middle-class family could become a multi-millionaire.

"But what about the poor guys?"

"If a poor man plans his expenses properly and manages to invest just ₹2,000 per month from a young age, say 22, he would accumulate almost ₹50 lakh by the time he turns 60.

So, even a poor guy can become a multi-millionaire. That's why it's called the magic of compounding."

Richard added, "the return assumed is around 10% post-tax in these calculations, which isn't possible with the traditional, fully taxable bank fixed deposits. Remember what Adaline Jones told you about proper asset allocation? With intelligent asset allocation, a 10% post-tax return on your overall portfolio is realistically possible and achievable."

After dinner, Richard called me to his room, and opening an iron safe from its far corner, removed a well-secured envelope. Then coming close to me, he said, "the tiniest of actions is always better than the boldest of intentions. And results always speak louder than words. So start budgeting for yourself today."

This time, the small memento that came with the envelope was that of a picture of a cute piggy bank and a young girl dropping a dollar into its wide mouth.

Pay Yourself First

Budget money for the things that you require, otherwise very soon you will be forced to sell the things that you need.

The things that are hardest to do are often for the best. Luck is where skill meets persistence. Success lies in maintaining masterful consistency around a few fundamentals. Change is hardest at the beginning, messiest in the middle and best at the end. While creating a *budget surplus*, for instance, you will initially ridicule yourself and people will make a mockery of you. However, if done consistently, persistently and patiently, it will make you lucky and help you attain financial nirvana. Small daily improvements and innovations lead to staggering achievements over time. Budget surplus should be a priority; paying yourself first should be seen as a compulsory expense, just like you pay tax to the government or loan instalments to the bank. Learn to delay gratification. Never spend more than you earn and also learn the difference between mere savings and real investments. Don't confuse saving with investing and do a proper asset allocation to generate a budget surplus. Don't just cut spending to be wealthy because thrift may allow you to accumulate some wealth but not make you wealthy – instead, spend your way to riches, by creating a proper budget surplus, which when allocated intelligently to a basket of investment assets, will make your money work for you by creating passive and portfolio income. Achieving financial independence is a process and budgeting is an integral part of it. The more you go to your limits, the more your limits will expand. It generally takes about a decade to become rich and when you have a decade of budgeting behind you, you will look like an overnight sensation to others.

Not Even Widows Like to Speculate

I left Richard's house early in the morning for Nairobi Airport and this time, I did not have to walk the distance. Not that I would have found this daunting, as I now knew the importance of budgeting my energy and conserving it till the last mile was covered. Similarly, in life, I understood the need for conserving my money for the future. I appreciated the significance of paying myself first by creating a budget surplus. I also knew the value of proper asset allocation of my budgeted amount.

It was time to move on to my next destination, Johannesburg, South Africa, where I would meet my teacher Mandisa Kruger – a young widow and a mother of two children. I felt sad to think of the cruel blow fate had dealt Mandisa.

How could God be so unkind?

Then I remembered Faline Cheong. She had told me that every person in this world is here to do his karma. Maybe Mandisa was paying off some karmic debt left over from her previous lives.

It was a three-hour, 40-minute flight from Nairobi to Johannesburg. The flight took off at 10.10 am and when I landed in Johannesburg airport, I noticed the clock at the airport showed 12.50 pm. Thank God the time difference between Kenya and South Africa was only an hour!

This was the 14th day of my journey in search of wisdom. Although I was tired and homesick, I was no longer filled with anxiety about getting back to work and earning money. Perhaps my recently acquired financial wisdom was making me more confident and relaxed.

Johannesburg was crowded. I could hear conversation all around me. A couple on vacation was planning the next day's itinerary, investment bankers were talking about stock issues, a couple of gold miners were discussing the rising price of gold and how hoarding and speculating in gold futures was earning them more money than their gold mining business. Yes, I had read that South Africa is the world leader in gold mining.

Suddenly, the young voice of a woman rose above the din. "Good afternoon, Mr John Pinto! I am Mandisa Kruger the keeper, teacher and preacher of the sixth financial commandment."

I turned around to see a tall and slender young woman in her late 20s. She was wearing long trousers, a long jacket with wide collars and low-heeled shoes. I couldn't help noticing her hour-glass figure.

"Why are you staring at me?" she asked. "I am a mother of two, an eight-year-old daughter and a five-year-old son. I am 29."

I was rather taken aback at her directness. What confidence she had to talk so fearlessly to a complete stranger.

She then led me to her car. "We are heading toward Sandton, which is where I live." I had never heard of this place before. On my enquiry, Mandisa replied, "Sandton was established in the late 60s as a semi-rural extension of Johannesburg, but in the past decade it has grown into a major commercial and financial center of Gauteng and South Africa. It is just 14 miles from the airport."

As if to show that I, too, was knowledgeable about South Africa, I quickly added, "I know that South Africa is also known as the 'country of gold', and gold is most precious as its value never goes down and is a good hedge against inflation."

She looked sharply at me and almost jamming the brakes said, "so you believe gold is the asset to possess as its value never comes down?"

"Yes," I replied confidently.

She laughed aloud. "Ok, let's examine this. Gold rose 23 times from US$35 in the year 1971 to US$850 by the year 1980, when the then US President, Nixon, removed the US from the gold standard and turned the US dollar into a currency that can be printed at the free will of the government without any backing of gold."

Without paying any heed to the latter part of what she said, I jumped in my car seat excitedly.

"That's what I was saying. Gold prices only go one way and that is up."

"You are too impatient. From US$850 in the year 1980, gold fell to US$250 by the year 2000, a staggering 70% absolute fall over a 20-year period."

"But I have only seen gold prices rise in India, even between the years 1980 and 2000. Still, you say it has fallen by 70%."

"That's the catch, my friend," Mandisa turned into a by-lane and then passed through the gate into the compound of her house.

She had an incredibly beautiful house with a swimming pool on one side and two garages on the other. The outside walls looked like they were made of stone. Mandisa took me on a tour of her large, four-bedroom duplex, comprising a large living room, kitchen and servant's quarters. The inside walls were elegantly painted in two contrasting colors, that gave the house a perfect look. The furniture looked imported and the kitchen was fully outfitted with the latest gadgets. The guest room was very spacious and well-laid out. I put my luggage on the floor and was ready to collapse on the bed. However, the heady smell of rich food wafting from the kitchen drew me to it.

"Good afternoon, ma'am," said a maid wiping her hands on her apron. "Lunch is ready to be served."

"And we are ready to eat," replied Mandisa looking at me. She then called out to her children, who appeared in a trice. I was soon introduced to beautiful Nomuula and the ever-smiling Larry.

The traditional South African spread included *biltong*, or strips of dried meat, and *potjiekos*, a deliciously slow-cooked meat and vegetable stew, which, I was told, was cooked over an open fire. Then, there was leg of lamb stuffed with bacon, garlic and rosemary, served with roast potatoes, green beans, pumpkin and cauliflower cheese, as well as roast chicken.

Mandisa told me how South Africans love their *braais* (barbecues) T-bone steaks, *boerewors*, lamb and pork chops, as well as a variety of *sosaties* and *potjiekos*. Like the *braai*, *potjiekos,* too, are a social event where family and friends gather outdoors around an open fire and cook up a delicious stew. The three-legged cast iron pot that is used is basically the same as what was used in the old days. The *potjie* meal is often served with salads, rice and home-baked bread on the side, besides a traditional dessert. Mandisa concluded by announcing that the cast iron pot would be set up in the backyard that night. "We South Africans are very passionate about our food, just the way you are passionate about your gold."

Oh my god, I had forgotten about gold in the midst of this discussion of food. "Indian gold prices rose between the years 1980 and 2000, even when international gold prices fell. How was that possible?"

"That's very simple," she said. "In what currency would people buy gold in India?"

"Of course, the Indian rupee."

"Exactly, and in what currency is gold measured internationally?"

"US dollar."

"You are right. Now the question is, when you buy gold in India, which is world denominated in US dollars, in Indian rupees, what happens?"

As I scratched my head for an answer, she replied, "the US dollar gold gets converted to Indian rupee gold. That means you feel the effect of the exchange rate between the US dollar and the Indian rupee. In short, keeping the US dollar gold price constant, the weaker the Indian rupee against the US dollar, the higher the price of gold in Indian rupees. So, while on the one hand international gold prices fell from US$850 to US$250 between the years 1980 and 2000, on the other, the Indian rupee depreciated from ₹8 to ₹45 against the US dollar during the same period, leading to a bull market in Indian rupee-denominated gold prices. Therefore, it was not gold that was rising, but the Indian rupee that was depreciating. To sum up, it would have been much better for an Indian investor to buy US dollars instead of gold during that period."

What a revelation this was. The Indian currency had depreciated and I thought gold had appreciated! She was right. It would have been better to buy US dollars and hold it, rather than gold, because gold was at an artificially high level in India only because the rupee had weakened. As I mulled over these ideas, the table was filling up with a variety of puddings rich in butter, cream, sugar and spices.

After a heavy meal, Mandisa suggested that I rest while she taught her children.

I was woken up by the gentle, but firm voice of Mandisa. I followed it into her study. It was a spacious, neatly kept room with a big table in the middle. There were also two small folding tables and fitted chairs hanging from the wall.

"Are you ready for your lesson?" she asked. "Only when you are ready to learn will the master appear before you."

"In this case, a mistress," I said naughtily.

Ignoring my cheap comment, Mandisa pointed to a chair to her right. Her children were seated to her left.

A hot cup of coffee, nutty wheat buttermilk biscuits and milk tarts appeared before me. I noticed how Mandisa showed the utmost patience while teaching her children and did not just scold them for genuine mistakes. She used live examples and illustrations to clarify difficult concepts. Her manner was most engaging and it was clear she wanted to ensure the children would remember what they had learned all their lives.

"How I wish all teachers and parents were like you," I said impressed with her approach.

"Actually, the fault lies not with the teachers or parents, but with our education system, which is based on the system of elimination. The focus is not on advancing the stronger ones, but on holding back the weaker ones. It puts the dangerous idea in the tender minds of young children that for someone to win in this world, someone else must lose. It makes them believe that there isn't enough for everyone to win. It's an attitude borne out of the fear of scarcity. Instead of teaching them to work in harmony, the education system actually creates rivalry, jealousy and hatred among children."

This was quite an extraordinary perspective.

"Rather than developing the very best in each and every person, the system has conveniently pitted people against each other in this wild game of education, where there is nothing but the survival of the fittest," Mandisa continued.

"And the irony is that in this game of winners and losers, the winners also lose because they acquire their degrees by defeating fellow students in exams, but lack the knowledge, understanding, wherewithal and the wisdom to face this world. They learn about medicine, law, accounting, marketing, etc., but not about money. They win the insignificant test of school, but lose the all-important exam of life."

Her words were prophetic. After all, I was a living example of this twisted educational system. I was a great success academically, but an utter failure in life. Although these thoughts saddened me, the fact that I now had the opportunity to meet such an amazing teacher who was also my chosen mentor for imparting financial wisdom, filled me with joy.

"Continuing with your education on gold," Mandisa suddenly changed the topic, "the price of gold depends on the value of the US dollar, since gold is internationally quoted in US dollar. The weaker the dollar, the higher the price of gold and vice versa; the lower the real interest rates on US dollar denominated assets, the higher the price of gold and vice versa; and the weaker the home currency against the US dollar, the higher will be the domestic price of gold and vice versa."

"Do you know that gold is a speculative item?" she asked. Clearly, I didn't, so she went on to explain.

"Why do you invest?"

"For profits, of course."

"Right, that's true for most people. And that is why they end up making losses."

I was flummoxed. What a strange paradox – people making a loss, because they invest for making a profit.

"When you invest for profits, you are, in effect, investing for asset income. But when you invest for cash flow, you are investing for running income. And as the name suggests, running income is the income which keeps running throughout, in good times and in bad."

"So what do you mean by asset and running income? I have never heard these terms before."

"Running income is the current realized income from an investment asset during its lifetime," came the immediate answer. "Hence, if the investment is dissolved to derive some kind of income then this would not be running income. Examples of running income would include dividend on shares, interest on bonds, rent on real estate, etc.

In contrast, asset income is nothing but the return on your assets. While running income is derived as a return on your assets during the asset's lifetime, asset income is the return from investments as a consequence of the asset itself, either partly or fully being liquidated and sold. Examples of asset income would be the profits made from the sale of equity shares, bonds, real estate, etc.

Now, let me ask you this simple, but all important question. For what should you invest, running income or asset income?"

I was clueless and recognizing that, Mandisa continued, "I would certainly advise you to always invest for running income, because that gives you continuous income without sacrificing the investment itself. While for earning asset income, you have to sell, partly or fully, the asset itself. To take an example, if you have a chicken, you can get an egg from it every day. This would be your running income or you could just cut up the chicken and eat it and this would be your asset income. Therefore, always invest for running income. If asset income is generated along with it, then well and good, but don't invest for that. And remember, a cardinal principal of investment is that if you truly invest for running income, then it's only a matter of time before that also generates asset income. This is because when you invest for running income, you would be buying value and that's something that invariably gets rewarded over a period of time through an increase in asset price. And when you invest for running income, you are, in effect, investing for cash flow. Therefore, here you're not concerned with the intermittent increase or decrease in the value of the asset. But if you invest for asset income, you are more concerned with an increase in the value of the asset, because only then will you earn a return from your investment."

As I tried to comprehend the difference between running and asset income, she continued, "when you buy gold, you are actually buying it for asset income, because gold doesn't produce any kind of cash flow or running income. On the contrary, it produces negative cash flow in the form of holding costs, storage costs, wealth tax, etc. And any investment which produces only asset income is nothing but a speculative item."

I was so engrossed in absorbing these ideas – running income, asset income, cash flow and return on investments, that I didn't notice her children had completed their evening assignments and were done with their class.

As promised, Mandisa had the cast iron pot set up in her backyard for the evening. "The traditional cuisine of the Afrikaner community stems from the Dutch, French and

German settlers, who founded the Cape colony in South Africa. Their descendants today are called Africans. Besides grilling over an open fire, the Voortrekkers often made a stew of venison and whatever vegetables they could find, in a three-legged cast iron pot. Hence, the name *potjiekos* or potfood. As they led physically demanding lives, the Voortrekkers, and later the Boers, favored robust foods. But over time, some things have changed. Lighter meals with plenty of salads, chicken, and fish have become popular in urban Afrikaner homes nowadays. However, South Africans remain as fond as ever of their *braai* or barbecue. "

That night, I ate the heavy pot food and went to bed, hoping to digest the food, as well as the wisdom.

I got up the next morning with a fire in my belly to learn more from my awe-inspiring teacher. After our morning sugary cuppa and rusk (a hard cookie and butter bread), Mandisa and I were ready to visit an ongoing art exhibition in the city.

The art gallery had both ancient and modern art. The exterior design of the gallery, with round dome and square base, symbolized the ancient idea of a round heaven and a square earth. It was divided into 11 segments and three exhibition halls. There were all kinds of art on display at ridiculous prices, yet there were plenty of buyers. We also visited the auction hall and I was shocked to hear the prices being offered for some of the paintings that made little sense to me.

"Do you know who most of these buyers are?" Mandisa asked, suddenly.

"Obviously, true lovers of art."

"Actually, there's nothing so obvious here," she said. "Most are investors, or more accurately speculators, who buy these paintings for asset income, hoping they can sell an absurd, meaningless painting at an even higher price to some equally silly person."

"The greater fool theory," I jumped in excitement.

"Yes, you're right," she said agreeing with me for probably the first time. "And once the greater fool disappears, the last person left holding the art, which he believes is an investment asset but in reality is nothing but a speculative item, actually becomes the greatest fool."

I sheepishly remembered all those times I had also invested, or rather speculated, in such absurd and costly items, on which there was no running income, only to eventually lose all my money.

That afternoon, Mandisa treated me to lunch in a nice Indian restaurant in Johannesburg, where I got to have my favorite mutton biryani, besides Indian curry and naan. I felt so indebted to Mandisa, both for her wisdom and her hospitality.

That evening we planned to visit a club, which she said held special sentimental value for her. I forgot the name of the club, but remembered it was a very happening place where the who's who of South Africa, elite businessmen, high-flying professionals, movie stars and sports personalities congregated.

I said somewhat jealously, "Mandisa, you're lucky to be a member of such a famous club. The value of this investment will keep increasing even as you enjoy its benefits and amenities."

"Investment? You mean a club membership is an investment?"

"Of course. A club membership, particularly of such a posh club, is an investment whose value will go up year after year as more potential members bid for higher and higher prices."

Mandisa burst out laughing. "Club membership fees may run into thousands or even cross millions. While it may be good for your social life or sometimes business connections, it's not an investment asset. It's merely an unnecessary revenue expenditure.

Although, some will argue that it's a life membership and therefore, an asset for life," she second-guessed my protestations, "I would like to ask such people one question: just because it is life membership, how does it become an asset? Is it going to generate running income for life? If not, how can it become an investment asset? In fact, clubs will incur recurring unnecessary revenue expenditure in the form of expenses on food, games, tournaments, events, functions, etc., all of which will rob you of your hard-earned money."

Not convinced, I continued to argue. "Since the value of a club membership rises year after year, it should be considered an asset."

Taking a sip of water, she countered, "even if the value rises, can you realize it? Can you sell it and get back your money? If you can't, how can it be your investment asset? Just because some bigger fool has paid more money than you, this does not in any way turn the club membership from an unnecessary revenue expenditure on a speculative item into an investment asset. For any asset to pass the litmus test of an investment asset, it must generate positive cash flow in the form of running income. A club membership is in no way close to doing that. Furthermore, the perceived value of such a membership cannot, at any point of time, be actually realized by you, simply because it's not a saleable commodity. So a club membership is a great cash flow–producing investment asset in the books of the club, not yours."

I was astonished at the sagacity of this lone, young widow and mother of two young children. But one thought that kept bothering me was what had prompted her to take up such a costly club membership.

"It was not me but my late husband. Whenever I come to this club, I feel a sense of pride as this was bought by my husband with his own money. At the same time I do feel distressed about the grave financial mistake he made. However, this was relatively small compared to some other money mistakes he made."

Sensing my eagerness to know the whole story, she said, "my husband was a gold retailer. He owned a shop in one of the jewelry markets of Johannesburg. He used to make a small, but decent margin in gold retailing. However, it was not long before the speculative bug bit him and he started speculating in gold, silver, diamond and platinum. He started hoarding these speculative items, hoping their prices would increase, by creating negative leverage. He also held huge open positions in these speculative items through derivative contracts in the financial markets. He was no longer interested in the retail margin, that is, the running income from his gold retailing, but wanted to profit from the increase in the price of those commodities, that is the asset income for which he used even debt by creating negative leverage. A time arrived, as it eventually comes, when the price of these commodities fell. His potential asset income turned into huge asset losses and on top of that, the negative leverage multiplied his loss. He became so indebted, that he had to liquidate his actual gold retailing business to pay off his losses. In short, he became bankrupt, losing not only his money, but also his confidence. Feeling trapped, he resorted to the cowardly act of suicide, leaving me and my young children to fend for ourselves alone in this big bad world."

At this point, she broke down, but being the courageous lady she was, she soon recovered to continue her tale of woe.

"Amid the incessant ringing of the doorbell by creditors and bankers, I remembered Vijay Desai, to whom I had sold some gold jewelry on one of his visits to this city. Impressed with my knowledge of financial concepts, he had said that if I ever needed his help, I shouldn't hesitate to call. The great humanitarian that he is, Vijay not only cleared my debts, but also shared with me his ten financial commandments. He inspired confidence in me to start a consultancy here in Johannesburg to help people become financially free."

As I ate dinner that day in that posh club, I gave silent thanks to God for saving me from the brink of suicide and for bringing me in contact, once again, with Vijay Desai. I marveled at how Vijay had chosen my mentors carefully, ensuring each one's life embodied the wisdom they had been instructed to share with me. In my mind, I bowed in gratitude to my dearest friend and promised myself that I would repay my debt of gratitude to him by passing on the knowledge I was acquiring to others.

The next morning I was up earlier than usual, as Mandisa, I and her two incredible kids were headed to the Kruger National Park. We boarded a flight from Johannesburg to Kruger Mpumalanga International Airport, located in the southern corner of the park. I was really thrilled when I entered Kruger National Park. Lying in the heart of the Lowveld is this wildlife sanctuary inviting visitors to immerse themselves in the unpredictability and endless wilderness that is the essence of Africa. Nearly 2,000,000 hectares of land stretch 352 kilometers from north of South Africa, to just south of Zimbabwe and west of Mazambique.

This is the land of baobabs, fever trees, knob thorns, marula and mopane trees underneath which lurk the Big Five, the Little Five and the birding Big Six. There are four zones in the park: the central zone is home to such animals as the lion, leopard, hyena, cheetah, zebra, wildebeest and elephant; the far north region is for birds and reptiles along the river flood plains; the north region is defined by unvarying shrub mopane thriving in hot low-lying valleys where the hippo, buffalo, impala and elephant thrive; and the southern region is home to the Crocodile River and the highest point in the park, Khandz alive.

"So is this is the largest park in the world?" I asked.

"Yes. It covers 20,000 square kilometers."

"What a wonderful asset the government has," I sighed. "I wish I, too, had some land as investment."

"You believe land is an investment?"

"Yes, of course."

"So, what running income does land give you?"

I was tongue-tied. The car came to a halt as we reached the southern part of the park, where our trekking would begin. The dirt path was narrow and twisted, and it started to climb almost instantly. As we plodded on, I felt like I was mounting shallow stairs, many times stepping on a tree root or boulder. The valleys were home to trees rarely found in other parts of the Kruger Park, such as the Cape chestnut, coral tree and lavender fever-berry. The underground granite produced distinctive smoothed koppies at irregular intervals, which were typically surrounded by rock figs and were ideal places to spot rock daisies or hyrax, baboon and klipspringer, even the odd leopard.

As we moved through the wild, I was still trying to articulate why I thought land was an investment asset and what the running income from it was. Noticing my face tensing, Mandisa volunteered to resolve my dilemma. "There is no running income from land. On the contrary, there are running expenses on it such as property tax, maintenance, keeper's wages, utility bills, etc. When you buy land, you are buying it for asset income, to flip it and sell it to a buyer at a higher price. So, land isn't an investment asset, but a speculative item."

Although I had read so many stories of people going bankrupt investing in land, I had never thought of it as being a speculative investment.

"But land yields products, both agricultural produce and minerals," I persisted.

"You are right, John," Mandisa explained. "When you hold land to get any kind of produce from it, like farm output, minerals, oil, etc., you are using land as a fixed asset for your business, in the same way as an industry uses machinery to produce its final product. In this case, you aren't holding land so as to sell it at a higher price, but as a means to produce goods in which you trade. In fact, in such cases, the intention is never to sell the land, because land is like the cow that gives you milk every day. The idea is to ensure the daily supply of milk and not to slaughter the cow."

What an interesting example. I knew the analogy would stay with me forever.

The view from the top of Khandz alive was beautiful, with the Crocodile River to the south, the Sabie River to the north and the jagged ridges of the Lebombo mountains visible in the distance, but this stunning scenery was just the icing on the cake – the cake was the financial wisdom I was gaining in this extraordinarily wild place.

That evening we camped out in one of the bush lodges. Over a campfire barbecue, we met an interesting retired American couple who had come on holiday to South Africa. Noticing that both Mandisa and I were from the fast-growing BRICS (Brazil, Russia, India, China and South Africa) countries he talked about how, lately, the US dollar had strengthened against all major currencies, including the Indian rupee and the South African rand. He wanted to know if it was time to sell the US dollar and buy emerging market currencies in the hope of some rebound. Mandisa responded by saying she would never invest or take a bet on any currency. It was not an investment asset, but a rather dangerous speculative item which gets traded 24 hours for 365 days and whose value depends on the ever-changing unpredictable macro-environment in the world economy. "How can somebody sitting in one corner of the world predict what will happen to global growth, inflation, interest rates, government finances, Central Bank actions, current account and trade balances, fiscal balances and government actions in every other country," she asked.

"It's not just difficult but almost impossible. So all investments in currencies are purely speculative in nature. And, in any case, you're being exposed to this speculation indirectly when holding an international asset like foreign equity/bond or any commodity quoted in an international currency, like gold, which gets valued in US dollar terms. So there's no need to buy and hold a currency, which doesn't yield any running income, and in the process overexpose yourself to a speculative item, like currency," she told him. Having gained wisdom on land, metals, minerals and currencies, I had a peaceful and enlightened sleep in the wild.

Next morning, I woke up to the sound of birds singing and small animals scurrying across the forest floor. I felt invigorated and decided to get some physical exercise. The only real exercise I had since embarking on this journey was the walk, the mountain climb that I had taken with Richard Omondi and the trek the day before in the Kruger National park. I put on my track pants and shoes and went out to jog a short distance in the woods. Back in the camp, I did a round of push-ups, sit-ups and squats.

I caught Mandisa watching me from a distance. "Exercise is an insurance policy you have taken for your health and each day you pay a premium by going to the gym. Good health is a medal on the neck of a healthy person that only a sick person will notice," she said. I gave myself a pat on the back on hearing this.

That day we drove to the central region of the park, full of sweet grasses and abundant browsing trees, which supported large groups of antelope, zebra, wildebeest, and giraffe, along with half of the park's population the lion, leopard, cheetah and hyena.

I finally summoned the courage to ask Mandisa the question that had been on the tip of my tongue all morning. "You are so young and beautiful, have you never thought of a second marriage. A father for your two kids, a companion for yourself?"

She took a deep breath before replying. "A second marriage is a big risk like a derivative. What if my second husband ill-treats my children, especially if we have our own children? What if my second husband does not understand me the same way my first husband did? And being a widow there is a very strong possibility that I might have to marry a divorcee. I could also end up being one, for if a man can't live with one woman, then he probably can't live with any woman. And if these problems surface, my marriage would become like a financial derivative. Just as a derivative instrument multiplies the gains or losses and has the potential to wipe out an investor's entire capital if it goes against him, my second marriage too, if it goes wrong, would multiply my problems and completely ruin my and my children's lives.

So, although I agree with you that everyone needs company in this world, that need not always be the spouse, it can also be a good friend. Always choose your friends wisely, making sure they are people who will inspire you to be true to yourself."

Later, we visited the far north and the northern part of the park, before heading back to Johannesburg by road. For the first 50 miles or so, the road wound its way through the edge of the park as it circled the coast. Then it got enveloped by deep green hills on either side. We crossed several villages on our journey. Along the way, I saw some beautiful bungalows and houses with lush gardens. What a perfect weekend retreat these would make, I thought.

"These posh bungalows and houses would make great investments, wouldn't they," I offered.

"I thought by now you would know the difference between an investment asset and a liability disguised as an accounting asset. Do any of these posh bungalows yield running income? On the contrary, the more fancy the bungalow, the higher would be the running costs incurred to maintain it. Then how on earth can those be seen as investment assets?" came the sharp retort.

I instantly realized my folly and looked away in shame.

Once back in Mandisa's house, we settled down for dinner after which she came to me with a packet. Handing it over, she wished me goodnight and retired to her room with her children.

When I opened the packet, I noticed an envelope along with a small memento that carried a picture of a man standing with his feet on two rocks, one covered with fire and the other one with ice. I instantly understood its meaning – speculation was like simultaneously placing your feet on fire and ice. Without wasting any more time, I silently opened the envelope.

Invest, but Don't Over-invest, in Speculative Items

You should be investing in speculative items but overdoing it will leave you with an investment hangover.

It takes only a moment to break what takes a whole life to make. To earn money use your brains, but use your heart to preserve and grow it. Invest in assets that produce running income and let asset income just flow as a by-product of it. Speculative assets yield only asset income as they are incapable of generating running income. Life is speculative as you don't know what turn it will take and whether your most precious assets, including your loved ones, will be with you or not; the same goes for speculative items. So lead life fearlessly with confidence, nurturing adversity as it breeds opportunity, increasing your allocation for speculative items during cyclical lows and reducing exposure at close to cyclical peaks. Just as being physically fit increases your chances of fighting physical attacks, gaining knowledge of and acquainting yourself with different commodities, currencies, art and other speculative items, multiplies your odds of success with them. Managing money is not about doing the things that you like, but rather about doing the things that are right. Therefore, you should be allocating money to speculative items but in limited quantities keeping in mind the asset and investment cycle within your overall asset allocation.

Equities – Your Share of Profits

I spent a restive night before taking the morning flight to New York. Yes, I was moving from South Africa, the land of wilderness, to the United States of America, the world's most industrially developed nation.

After a super South African breakfast onboard the flight, I pondered over my incredible journey of the past two weeks and the lessons I had received from the many incredible people I had met and befriended. It was a really long flight of a little over 17 hours. I was glad for the memories that kept me busy thinking about all I had learned, while my enthusiasm about my next stop kept me excited.

Finally, I landed in New York, the financial capital of the richest country in the world. As I alighted, I noticed it was evening, probably around 5 pm. Waiting outside the airport gate was a charming, middle-aged, tall and broad-shouldered man in shining spectacles, waving frantically at me. As I approached him, he thrust his hand forward and said, "welcome to New York, Mr John Pinto. I am Mark Adams, your new teacher, who will demystify for you the intriguing world of equity investments."

My initial reaction was that I already knew all about equity investments. And then I recalled the number of times I had lost money in the stock markets, they easily outnumbered the number of times I had made anything; the number of times I had bought high just before the crash or sold low just before the next big upturn; the many occasions on which I had invested in the next great idea or story, only to be taken for a ride by the promoter; the countless instances when my paper investments had turned out to be just paper, utterly worthless.

I suddenly realized I was sitting beside Mark Adams in his car and being driven to, I assumed, his residence.

"Where do you stay?"

"Brooklyn."

The name sounded familiar.

Mark smiled. "It is known to many as New York City's favorite and most well-known borough. Brooklyn has been the subject of so many books and movies that even if you've never been there, you would recognize it."

We passed over bridges and through a tunnel. At certain places, I saw people risk their lives to cross the busy roads. Responding to my gesticulations of frustration, Mark said, "be it life or dealing with equity investments, the major hurdle to success is not being able to delay gratification. If you seek overnight success, you are surely asking for disaster."

So, is the pedestrian who takes some risk to cross the road ahead of others, deserving of praise?

"This is an unwarranted risk they are taking. The same way, many investors don't realize what they are doing when they blindly invest in stocks. Investing in costly, but sound, proven businesses with quality management isn't the chief risk confronting an average investor; rather, it is the buying of cheap stocks of dubious companies that is the main hazard."

Looking at my blank face, he continued, "why do you invest in stocks?"

"Obviously for profit."

"And where does the profit come from?"

"From the difference between the selling price of stock and its purchase price."

"Do you know why the stock price goes up?"

"Because the market goes up."

"And why does the market go up?"

"Because everybody expects the market to go up," I offered lamely.

Mark smiled. "A stock or the overall market goes up or down because of two factors: change in earnings and change in the valuation of those earnings. Generally, as a thumb rule, stock prices are positively correlated with earnings growth and vice versa. The valuation of those earnings are correlated with the expectation of a change in those earnings. If expectations are positive, then valuations will be high and vice versa."

As I thought about this, he continued, "stocks or markets are valued based on a certain multiple, which is called the price/earnings multiple. For example, if a stock earning ₹10 per share is quoted at ₹150, it means that it is being valued at 15 times its earnings. Now, the return can come from two things. Say, the earnings increase to ₹12 per share and the valuation remains constant at 15 times, the price will move up to ₹180. Now, say, the earnings remain constant at ₹10 per share, but the market starts valuing it at 20 times, the stock price will move up to ₹200. This earnings-valuation matrix can work in as many combinations as you can imagine, but this is the basic premise of it."

Earnings, growth in earnings, price/earnings valuation multiple and change in the valuation multiple, this man was already impressing me with his knowledge.

"You should also take into account dividends while taking your investment decision, because that is what you will receive while you hold the stock," he observed.

"Who cares about small dividends, when I can earn so much more from capital gains in stocks," I retorted.

"Good blue chip stocks are fountains of dividends, and offer as much, if not more, investment growth potential than less stellar companies, but carry far less risk. In equity investing, there is no substitute for quality. Understanding the health of a company is not limited to looking at its profits, but extends logically to dividend payouts because, unlike a profit which is just an accounting entry, dividend is the actual cash which the company has to pay its shareholders."

This was news to me, as I had never really given dividends the importance I had given stock prices.

"The return which an equity investor gets over his holding period is determined by three factors," Mark continued. "The initial dividend yield, growth in earnings and change in the valuation multiple."

Just then, we passed through the gates of his housing society. We rang the doorbell of his apartment and a young girl of 12 greeted us. There was another girl of about seven behind her. Mark introduced them as Susan and Karen, respectively.

Mark's house was beautifully done up, with the furniture and wall-mounted units showing intelligent use of the apartment space. Everything seemed to be in place and in perfect harmony.

The lady of the house must be taking very good care of the house. I looked around to see if I could spot her, but there was no sign of anyone else. Suggesting that I rest after my long flight, Mark showed me to my room: a small, compact place that had been kept very neat and tidy. I rested for a while, although I no longer felt as tired, or suffered as much jet lag as before, and could get up and sleep at any time I wanted.

After a short nap and shower, I made my way to the kitchen drawn by the sound of utensils. To my utter surprise, I saw young Susan, busy cooking while standing on a small stool. "You are a brave and talented girl," I told her. "Are you not afraid of hurting yourself?"

Stirring the vegetables in the pan, she said philosophically, "whether dealing with life or equities, one must be aware of the risks one is taking and be brave enough to carry out one's plan."

Oh God, the daughter seems as knowledgeable about equity investments as the father!

"Are you learning cooking or equity investments from my daughter?" I heard Mark's voice from the far end of the dining room. I immediately headed toward him and smiled. As we made ourselves comfortable at the dining table, Karen, the younger daughter, laid out the table. Soon Susan came in with the food – fresh sweet corn fritters, lemon and yogurt marinated grilled chicken, beefy shepherd's pie with feta, and red onion and tomato salad. The culinary skills of this young girl were simply unbelievable.

As we tucked into the feast prepared for us, Mark continued with his lessons. "When you buy stock, you are simply buying a part of the business of the company. Remember, great fortunes on the stock market are made not by buying stocks, but by selling stocks of your own company. After all, it is the entrepreneurs, who have created substantial value in their companies, who are now selling stock that they got almost free, for a price. They create valuable businesses and then sell shares of ownership in the business to others."

Oh! So that explained why those lists of the super-rich rarely included names of investors, but were usually flooded with names of the promoters and owners of businesses.

"There are five major factors which affect the price of any tradable instrument including equities – macroeconomic, monetary, fundamental, technical and psychological factors. Macroeconomic factors are very important in the initial stages of an investment cycle. One must know whether one is in a structural bull or bear market, and this can be determined by looking at macroeconomic factors such as GDP growth, inflation, fiscal deficit, etc. However, equity investments cannot be based just on macroeconomic factors, because the stock market is the barometer of the economy and it predicts the macroeconomic factors some six to nine months before they come into play. Therefore, as far as macroeconomic factors are concerned, one must invest in stocks when the situation moves from bad to worse and not wait till it turns good, because by then stock prices might have rallied substantially from their bear market lows."

Even as I tried to get my head around this explanation, Mark continued tirelessly, "the second factor would be monetary conditions. For example, high interest rates are one of the biggest enemies of equities because they are likely to result in a fall in corporate earnings through increased interest costs, reduction in equity valuations like the P/E multiple through an increase in the discount rate, and by making available less investor surplus for equities as it makes debt attractive. An investor cannot wait for all monetary factors to become good before buying. They must invest when they believe interest rates are close to peak or will rise slightly, because that is the time when the worst, as far as this factor is concerned, has played out.

The third factor is related to the fundamentals, such as earnings, sales, book values, etc. on which stock prices and valuations should ideally be based, as these are the factors on which an entrepreneur or owner will value his business enterprise.

"The fourth factor," he went on, "is technical analysis, which practically begins where fundamental factors end. Once investors decide what to buy, they have to ascertain when to buy and when to sell. Technical analysis is nothing but predicting the future by looking at past trends."

"The fifth and final factor," he added, "is the psychological factor, because this is what separates the successful investor from the novice. Whatever one's investment method, the important and differentiating point is to follow it and be psychologically strong and sound to apply it practically. I quote Sir John Templeton over here, who said that 'to buy when others are despondently selling and sell when others are greedily buying, requires the greatest fortitude and pays the greatest reward' – this quote explains the psychological factor in a nutshell."

My dessert of fresh fruits and plain vanilla ice-cream came with another dollop of wisdom from Mark.

"Whether it is ice-cream or equity investments, plain is always better than flavored. Always invest in index or be as close to it as possible, because it is simply very difficult to beat the index over the long term, and if you can't beat it then better be part of it."

Before retiring to my room for the night, I peeped out of the window to see a city abuzz with life. Then I looked up – every passing moment seemed to turn the sky a shade deeper and the full moon looked like a giant pearl hanging from it. I suddenly remembered my family and sighed as I got ready for bed.

I was up at six the next morning, an hour later than usual. I wasn't happy to find I had robbed myself of one hour from my life. Mark's house was bursting with activity. Susan was busy preparing the breakfast, while little Karen was laying out the table, and Mark was dusting the furniture. Again, strangely, the lady of the house was nowhere to be seen.

"Hey John," Mark shouted. "Freshen up quickly, your breakfast is getting cold." Soon I joined Mark and Karen at the dining table, as Susan served us Sloppy Joes (a sandwich served with cheddar croutons and oatmeal chocolate fudge and authentic espresso café).

I asked Mark if equity investments are for the long- or short-term. He looked straight into my eyes and answered, "neither."

"While it is true that equity investments are primarily for the long term, all asset classes move through cycles. You have to buy equities, or for that matter any asset class, during cyclically low valuations and sell them in cyclically high-price periods. Understanding economic and business cycles is of paramount importance. As a general rule, first bond prices go up as interest rates come down, then equities enter a bull market and finally commodities blossom. That is the key to get above-average return from equities."

Taking a sip of coffee, he continued, "the US Dow Jones Industrial Average has returned a compounded growth of 5.2% over the past 117 years, since its inception in 1896. However, during this long period, there have been at least five instances when it has multiplied anywhere between two to five times in a matter of a few years. But there have also been few instances when it has not returned any money for long periods of time, like 15 to 40 years, which can be the full investment lifespan of an individual. That is what I meant by investing at cyclically low valuations and selling in cyclically high-price periods."

After breakfast, Mark took me to the neighborhood gym. "Just as cardio and weight training are exercises for the body and knowledge is exercise for the mind, so is investments exercise for your money – it makes it grow and stay healthy," Mark observed.

He made me run on the treadmill for about 15 minutes, followed by push-ups, stomach crunches, squats and biceps curls. I enjoyed this exercise routine. "While exercise removes unwanted fat and toxins from the body in the form of sweat and at the same time pumps blood and oxygen from the heart, proper investment monitoring helps remove all unwanted toxic investments from the portfolio."

I wondered how many investors in the world monitor their investments regularly. I know, I never did.

Mark pointed out that just as getting a well-toned body takes weeks, even months, of regular exercise, getting rich through equities was also not something that could be done overnight.

Just then, I was introduced to a gentleman named, Karl, who, I learned later, was the CEO of a mid-sized pharmaceutical company. "This man did not become the CEO of the company overnight or in a week or month, but after several years of learning, practice and work," Mark said. "So how can a boy just out of college without any experience hope of becoming a success in the equity markets?

And it's not how hard you work, but how smart you work that matters in life and in the markets. Always learn to be patient, disciplined and pragmatic in the market, listen to everyone, but have your own independent view, frame your own philosophy and methodology of investments and then be psychologically strong to follow it." Mark's words fell like pearls of wisdom on my ears.

Seeing me check my weight in the gym, Mark said, "the father of value investing, Mr Benjamin Graham, once observed that in the short run, the market is a voting machine, but in the long run it is a weighing machine."

As I lifted weights, Mark cautioned me not to hurt myself or anyone else.

"Aren't weights risky like equities?"

"Yes, blindly speculating in equities is a very big risk you are taking with your money, but investing after due research is the best thing you can do for your money.

Investing in equities is not actually risky over the long-term; it is just that the volatility over the short-term makes it look risky. Learn to distinguish between risk and volatility.

The biggest risk of all is that one fine morning you may get up and see that there is money in your bank, but that money cannot buy you the goods and services that you thought it would. That is the risk of inflation. The only thing which can protect you against inflation is commodities or equities, because as inflation raises the prices of goods, that is commodities, it also increases the earnings of many companies and consequently its stock price.

Just as there are many myths surrounding dieting and exercise, there are many myths about equities, which lead investors to commit serious mistakes in the market."

"What kind of mistakes?" I snapped.

"For example, trying to catch the top or bottom in a stock or the market, little realizing only a fool can do that."

I sure had been that fool on numerous occasions.

But Mark was not done. "There are many misconceptions about equities. Like believing the stock has already fallen so much and therefore, cannot fall further, or if a stock has fallen, imagining that it will come back and rise to the original price without any change in its fundamentals, or that the stock has already risen a lot and so, cannot rise further, disregarding the fact that the fundamental business is still growing and sound, or continuing to buy stocks even when the company performance is deteriorating and buying low-priced stocks, believing them to be cheap when, in fact, they may be very costly in valuation terms as their low price cannot be supported by earnings," he said, without catching his breath.

While I jogged on the treadmill, Mark kept up his lecture. "There are some people who don't believe in their abilities to invest, but judge their stock market performance by the price movement of their stocks – just because the stock price goes up, they believe they are right and if it goes down, they feel discouraged. And then there are some investors, who blindly follow some guru, but these so-called investment gurus cannot beat the market, simply because they make up the market and everybody can't beat everybody. For there to be one winner, there has to be a loser. And don't forget that the buyer and seller are always on the opposite side of the trade and they both mysteriously believe that they are right – but one of them is, in fact, wrong.

And one more thing," he hurriedly added. "In the stock market, analysis does not work, but the jobs of the analyst is always secure."

I felt like saluting this man for such extraordinary knowledge of equity markets.

"You are truly a guru, Mark," I said meaning every word from the bottom of my heart.

"Certainly not, my friend," replied Mark, humbly. "I am no investment guru, but just a student of investing."

"So you must have made a fortune in the stock markets."

His eyes turned misty, as he avoided replying to me and we went back to his house.

After a shower and a protein shake, offered to offset my supposedly strenuous workout in the gym, we were off to Mark's broker. I was eager to witness live action in the greatest stock exchange of the world.

He took me inside the broker's office and straight to the dealing room. There were probably around 20 of them, sitting side by side, attending to one or more calls at any point of time. Their fingers worked the keyboards frenziedly, as they continuously punched in client orders. A large LED television set on the wall was tuned into CNBC. There were numerous other terminals tuned into Bloomberg and Reuters. A dealer would sometimes chart a stock price history on Reuters and, at others, check out some corporate result on Bloomberg.

As I stood riveted by all this activity in the dealing room, Mark interrupted my thoughts.

"Never get carried away by activity. Know the difference between investing and speculating. An investor chases value, while a speculator chases stock price."

Although I nodded my head, my eyes remained glued to the screens and the price ticker moving up and down. Trying to grab my attention, Mark said, "in the stock market, a small percentage of people end up being successful in the long run, whereas a majority of the people, in spite of being successful in the short run, end up losing money in the long run."

This statement immediately attracted my attention.

Seeing my renewed interest, he continued, "the market is supreme and above everybody – no government, central bank, industrialist or operator can alter the primary trend of the market, they can only complicate the wave structure. Bull and bear markets run for several years. Therefore, determine the primary trend of the market and, generally, don't go against the primary trend. Putting excessive emphasis on recent past history, as opposed to rational reasoning, is a common judgment error in psychological experiments, as well as in the stock market. When opinions in the market are overwhelmingly unanimous, beware, because markets are famous for doing the unexpected."

I was all ears now and noticed Mark was completely oblivious of the constantly moving price ticker or the clearly excited CNBC host. He went on, "buy the stocks of companies that have shown consistent growth in earnings and make those goods and services that people cannot do without. Never invest or trade more than you can reasonably afford to lose. Put your stop loss at a logical, not convenient, place and always adhere to it. Cut losses and let profits run. Don't let a profit get converted into loss. Tips are for waiters and not investors. When in doubt, stay out. Don't invest on the basis of hope and never be sentimental about your stock."

After such a dose of stock market wisdom, I was more than happy at Mark's suggestion that we go to a nearby McDonald's. I bit hungrily into my favorite burger only to be stopped mid-track by Mark's question.

"So, what do you think is the business of McDonald's?"

Thinking Mark was in a mood to pull my leg, I continued chomping on my burger. "You probably think it is the burger business," he answered his own question.

I remained disinterested.

But what he said next left me stumped.

"They are actually in the real estate business."

"What did you say?" I asked, my mouth full of food. "Yes, my friend, McDonald's is the largest commercial real estate owner in the United States. Their business model is completely different from that of other food chain models, as they charge rent on the basis of sales. Apart from this, as in case of normal franchise business, they also charge franchise fees and marketing fees. They are actually in the real estate business. The only reason they sell hamburgers is because it yields the most revenue from which their tenants can pay them rent."

I was flabbergasted. What revelations I had on equity, business and money in a gym, a broker's dealing room, and now a McDonald's restaurant!

We returned to Mark's house to find both his daughters, Susan and Karen, quietly and diligently working on their studies.

"You are so lucky, Mark, to have such sweet, obedient and independent daughters. They must be so clever. I'm sure they will grow up to be fine professionals."

"Yes John, they are very bright and I am sure they will do very well in school and college. But education teaches people to be slaves of money, not masters of it. Education teaches children that failures are bad, but life is full of failures. Education labels a student a failure, instead of the circumstances. Education does not allow a person to learn from its mistakes when in life, one's biggest teachers are one's mistakes. Education teaches children to acquire degrees and keep working for money, while in reality one has to learn to make money work for oneself. Education teaches people to be puppets and always dependent – first on their teachers, then their degrees, their companies, their bosses and finally, the government and retirement plans. In short, education makes young students enter a vicious cycle of working hard for money, paying more in taxes, depending on other people for their livelihood and finally, on the government for their retirement. *It transforms people into lifelong slaves.* And I don't want my daughters to be slaves."

Mark was as sharp a critic of the education system as Mandisa Kruger. And both had a point to make. After all, I was a living example of the failure of the prevailing education system – a distinguished surgeon but a miserable failure in life.

"Always learn from your mistakes and failures," Mark persisted. "Learn to think like a businessman and investor. Learn to be a leader, not only with people and in society, but also with your money."

Everything he said made so much sense, yet there was something about his picture-perfect life that was unsettling. Where was his wife? I had to find out.

Mark told me that we would be visiting the Statue of Liberty that evening. We took a ferry from Battery Park to get to Liberty Island.

"The Statue of Liberty was a gift from the French people to the people of the United States as a symbol of the international friendship forged during the American Revolution. Currently, it is under renovation."

Then turning to look directly at me, he added, "just as this iconic structure is being strengthened to ensure it continues to stand for many more generations, one must evaluate one's portfolio regularly to ensure it remains well-balanced."

There, standing in front of the Statue of Liberty, I asked Mark about his wife. "Is she out of town on some official work?"

Mark was silent, as he struggled to rein in his emotions. His eyes rose to the height of the Statue of Liberty and then the whole story came tumbling out.

"John, I was a very bright student and a topper from one of the best management institutes in the world. I was offered a high-flying job as trader in one of the world's top investment banks. Billions of dollars were invested and traded at the press of a button. I put huge bets on different asset classes – stocks, bonds, commodities, currencies and real estate. I would get in and out of these assets at lightning speed. My career was very successful. It was then that I met Jenna, who worked as a phone operator in the same firm. We fell in love and were soon married. Then came our two lovely children. My position was improving, portfolio was increasing, bets were becoming more ambitious and my salary greater – my fame as a successful trader was spreading. But all the time spent away from my home had been time stolen from my family. Consequently, the love that was once there was gone. I pretended to be a good father, but that was only from the outside as my children never felt that way. Even while sitting next to them, I was never there. My mind was always pondering the markets and thinking about what my next big trade would be. I guess the truth was that I was an extraordinarily selfish man. I wanted to be rich and famous and in the bargain lost what was most precious to me."

He started weeping like a child and I put my hand on his shoulder. Taking a sip of water, he continued, "one day, my wife was gone. She returned to her parents' home. She never came back. What did come was the divorce notice from her lawyer. I was emotionally disturbed and mentally unbalanced. I lost some big trades of my company which eventually cost me my job. I went through a very bitter divorce and now raise my daughters single-handedly.

It was then that I realized that we grow the most from our difficulties and setbacks. These experiences were sent to me to clean up my act and move through it. Life's greatest hurts are in fact the glorious opportunities sent from the heaven for personal growth, positive transformation and regaining the purpose of one's life."

Taking a pause and looking more composed now, he continued, "it was during this time that I met Vijay Desai, who told me that 'the best way to cheer yourself up is to try to cheer somebody else up'. He encouraged me to use my knowledge about investments to fill the gap in our education system. It was on his advice that I took up lecturing to management and other students on equity investing and the benefits of it.

Life is like the markets. There are ups and downs and enough signals of what is to come, but people don't pay attention. Market generally moves in four different phases. The first phase is when there is good news, but the market begins to ignore it and starts going down – this is the beginning of the bear market. If inspite of incremental good news, the market shrugs it off and starts going down, it is the market's way of saying that the bull market has ended, the general underlying economic scenario is not as good as it seems by the incremental good news and so it has to go down to discount it.

The next phase is when there is bad news and the market listens to it and continues its downward journey. This is when the market is in the midst of a full-fledged bear market. Everything is gloomy. There is all kinds of bad news going around, such as an economic downturn, falling corporate sales and profitability, job losses, persistent high inflation, rising interest rates, economic scandals, increasing political and social unrest, etc. The third phase is when there is bad news, but the market refuses to fall further. This phase marks the death of the bear and the birth of the new bull. When even after incremental bad news the market refuses to fall further, it is the market's way of saying that it has fallen enough, has already discounted all the negative news, and going forward, things in the economy and the general business conditions are not as gloomy as the current negative news suggests. The fourth and last phase occurs when there is good news and market continues to go up. This phase is the normal, full-fledged bull market. Everything around looks good and rosy, businesses are making big money, companies are announcing huge expansions and acquisitions, government is collecting good funds by way of taxes, people have lots of money to spend, etc. The economic environment, business conditions and ground realities are all good – the full-fledged bull market is up and running."

That evening, at the Statue of Liberty, I acquired many new insights into the meaning of life, love, family, money and investments. As usual, we had dinner cooked by Susan and served by Karen, and my heart melted as I saw these two amazing children live their lives. I felt blessed that I still had my family with me and made a promise to myself that I would never stint on the time I gave them.

The next morning I got up realizing this was the 20th day of my unbelievable journey around the world in search of wisdom about life and money. As I entered the living room, I was greeted with an amazing sight. There was Mark dancing to music in the middle of the hall. He was wearing tiny boxers and a tight t-shirt that showed off his ripped body to good effect. His hair combed back stylishly, Mark was a picture of happiness and energy. I wondered how a man who had taken such hard knocks in life could still be so cheerful and enthusiastic.

As though reading my mind, he said, "John, happiness is a state within us. You have to be truthful to yourself, live fearlessly and always strive to be the best in whatever you do. Do the work for which God sent you to this planet and live the life which you were meant to live. Happiness is bound to flow within you."

Lowering the volume of his music, he turned serious and looking into my eyes said, "when I lost my wife, job and money, and was left alone with my two young daughters, it was like hitting the bear market bottom of my life. Generally speaking, bear market bottoms happen when bad things are happening and the worst things are being discounted by the market. By discounting the worst things during bad times, the market assumes that the companies will never recover again and by discounting the worst probabilities during bad times, life assumes that the person will never rebound again. But then a voice comes from within, from one's highest self, which gives one strength to get up and start running again. A person who holds his nerves during the bear market of life or a stock, is sure to attain great financial fortune along with true happiness. That is what I did. Today I am richer than before, have more spare time than before and am very happy with my two daughters. Yes, my wife is no longer with me, but perhaps that was the best thing to happen to us as both of us had to heal our wounds. Our souls had to be cleansed and, perhaps, parting was the best method for it. Sometimes, one has to have faith in the divine power that created and sent everyone here.

As far as markets are concerned, the signs of great bear market bottoms are commodity price stabilization, price control or inflation subsiding, improving economic news being ignored by the market, reduction in central bank-controlled interest rates, rally in government bond prices, followed by corporate bonds and rising volumes on strong market days or falling volumes on weak market days. The congruence of all or most of these factors signal the end of the bear market by sowing the seeds of a new bull market."

Mark went back to relate his ideas to life saying, "the problem is that whenever life presents one with its finest opportunities bundled as great problems, one doesn't see beyond the obvious. If during this time, one chooses to dismantle one's deepest worries and start moving straight in the direction of one's fears, one can move to higher and higher stages of personal freedom and individual greatness."

Just then Susan walked in with our breakfast of toast, butter, jam, freshly baked cashew and honey cookies, besides tea. While I eyed it longingly, Mark seemed to regard it as an unnecessary distraction.

Without skipping a beat, he continued, "if you believe that stock markets always move in the way they are supposed to, then you are greatly mistaken. Do you believe that even if you were somehow successful in valuing a company, the stock of that company would move toward that price, at least in the short to medium-term?

Stock prices are like a pendulum – they can go from unjustifiable pessimistic under valuation to extreme irrational over valuation. Never forget the last of the determinants of asset and stock prices, which are psychological factors. The great scientist, Sir Isaac Newton, correctly summed it up when he said that 'I can calculate the motions of heavenly bodies, but not the madness of people', and the great economist, John Maynard Keynes, echoed it when he said 'there is nothing so disastrous than to follow a rational investment policy in an irrational world'. The proof of these statements can be seen if one studies human behavior, mass psychology, behavior finance and the madness of crowds. The law of an organized, or psychological crowd is mental unity. The individuals composing the crowd lose their conscious personality when swayed by emotion and are ready to act as one, and be directed by dangerous crowd intelligence.

History is witness to the fact that financial markets are neither rational nor efficient, and any investment strategy that ignores this is doomed to fail. The market is not there to oblige any individual; it has its unique ways to isolate individual weaknesses and exploit them to the maximum."

Saying this, he disappeared into his bedroom only to return with something in his hand. Stretching it toward me, he revealed what he was holding with a chuckle.

I saw an envelope along with a small memento with the picture of the famous three monkeys – 'see no evil, hear no evil, speak no evil'. It did not take me long to understand the meaning behind the picture – never invest in any stock without properly seeing or studying it yourself; never invest in any stock by just listening to any tip; and never recommend any stock to anyone which you yourself are not sure of.

Understanding the True Value
of Equity Investing

You can neither hope to create real, sustainable, long-term wealth nor become a successful businessman unless you are a successful equity investor.

Don't make the mistake of ever believing that you know more about what's in your best interests than the source that created you. Move in the direction of your fear using the winds of adversity to set sail the ship of your life. A strong foundation at home sets you up for a strong foundation at work. Make patience a virtue in the stock markets. Learn to endure short-term pain for long-term gains. Recognize how to distinguish between good and bad quality stocks and businesses. Major losses to investors come from purchase of low-quality securities at times of favorable business conditions. Understand and appreciate the factors that drive stock prices. Identify the determinations of stock returns – dividend yield, growth in earnings and change in P/E valuations. Try to buy into high-quality, dividend-paying companies with prospects of earnings growth which might be temporarily going through problems due to an overall unfavorable business environment. Stick to good companies with strong balance sheets irrespective of the fact that they might have temporary problem of profitability. It's impossible for anybody to consistently beat the general markets on a long-term sustainable basis. Instead of listening to the blind claims of experts and gurus, listen to yourself. Knowledge about behavior finance, crowd psychology and socio-economic factors will help you become a better investor as well as a better human being. Don't commit the unpardonable financial crime of investing only in bonds to avoid risk because the biggest financial risk of all is inflation. While investors buy shares in companies, entrepreneurs actually sell shares in their companies. The five major factors that affect the price of equities (or any freely tradable instrument, such as bonds and gold) are macroeconomic, monetary, fundamental, technical and psychological factors. Know the difference between investing and speculating – *an investor chases value while a speculator chases price.* Also understand the difference between risk and volatility – equities might be volatile in the short term but provide higher returns with much less risk over the long term. Interest rates are the biggest enemies of equities affecting it through reduced earnings, lower sales, depressed valuations and lower liquidity. There are very important lessons to be learned from history and bear market bottoms. Markets, like life itself, have their own methods of finding and exploiting human weaknesses. There are certain common mistakes which human beings commit and investors make while investing in common stocks. Beware of them. Patience and persistence make an unbeatable combination for success – whether in life or with equities – so increase your financial literacy, make time your friend and equity investments your chosen medium for riches.

Looking to Your Own House

I was very sad to part from Mark and his two incredible daughters. The qualities they embodied, such as patience, perseverance, a fighting spirit and a never-say-die attitude, were as much the hallmarks of a successful human being as of a successful equity investor. I took the morning flight from New York to my next destination, London. As I made myself comfortable in the aircraft, I went over all that I had learned from Mark, such as the difference between investment and speculation; risk versus volatility; the determinants of equity values, such as initial dividend yield, earnings growth and change in P/E valuations; factors driving stock prices; the fact that entrepreneurs sell stocks in their companies, while investors purchase them; the investment cycle; lessons from bear market bottoms and investor psychology.

Soon, the flight touched down in London. The line at customs appeared to be never-ending, and the wait for my luggage seemed like an eternity. When I exited the airport, the local time was 8 pm. I was greeted by Brandon Smith, my new mentor. Brandon was probably in his early 50s and his white curly hair framed a pale, wrinkled face. He wore small round glasses and a dark coat.

After greeting me politely, he quickly led me to the parking lot. The car drive into the city was slow. We were surrounded by commuters, the crush of people, and the high-rise towers reminded me of Mumbai. As we moved through a landscape that was foreign, yet somehow seemed familiar, I realized that in this vast city of millions, I knew no one other than Brandon.

As we reached the high-rise building where Brandon lived, I noticed dozens of people in the crowded lobby. Some people were lined up near the security cabin; it looked like there was a party in someone's house. I noticed a small girl playing with her Barbie doll in one corner and an old gentleman smoking his cigar in another. The lobby reverberated with shouts, laughter, gossip, and smoke. We took the elevator to the 20th floor to Brandon's apartment. A lovely woman with a bubbly smile, probably in her late 40s, opened the door. Brandon introduced her as his wife, Lily.

Lily immediately took me on a tour of their house, showing me their living room, kitchen, their daughter, Natasha's bedroom, and their son, Samuel's, room. She also showed me her bathroom, which made me feel a little awkward. As I wondered where I would be put up, Brandon said, "currently, our son is away studying for his engineering degree. So you can take his room. And just in case you are wondering, what if my son were present? Let me explain. In that case, you would sleep with me in my room, while my wife would shift to my daughter's bedroom. If the guest were a female, she would sleep with my wife in the bedroom, while I would have shifted to my son's bedroom, and if the guests were a couple, we would have given them our bedroom and I would have moved to my son's, and my wife to my daughter's room."

Lily piped in, "it's not that we cannot afford a bigger house. But we don't want to waste our money by buying a house bigger than what our requirements merit, and waste money on a liability disguised as an accounting asset."

Just then, I heard a sweet, teen voice, "your own house is a bad capital asset and not an investment asset. It takes money from your pocket in the form of property tax, maintenance, society charges, utility bills and mortgage payments."

As I turned to see who it was, Brandon introduced his daughter, Natasha. She had long, blond hair, black eyes, a clear face and a perfect figure – a fine combination of beauty and brains.

"I've always seen a house as an asset," I said, almost to myself.

But Natasha's sharp ears had picked it up and she tore into me. "There are many items which are classified on the asset side of the balance sheet in conventional accounting. But that does not automatically make them assets. To be considered one, they will have to pass the litmus test for assets and that is, they should not take money from your pocket. A house takes money from your pocket in the form property tax, maintenance fees, utility bills, telephone bills, as well as mortgage charges.

Although a house is a bad capital asset, one must still aim to own one to avoid the unnecessary revenue expenditure of rent, which does not result in the creation of a productive investment asset," she continued. "Further, one's own house saves you from the hassle of having to keep searching for new rental houses, adjust to new surroundings, a new school, etc. Finally, time is the biggest and most important asset of all, and if you are wasting your time on all this, you are losing the most valuable asset and the one needed to create all other assets.

So if you are contemplating shifting to a bigger house without any real need for it, don't forget that owning a house entails two type of costs – one, in the form of property tax, maintenance, utility bills, mortgage payments etc., and two, in the form of the opportunity cost of not utilizing the same funds for actual investment assets."

How foolish I was to feel jealous of my friends, who bought bigger and bigger luxury houses, little realizing that they were just adding unnecessarily to their monthly bills.

Soon it was time for dinner and my mouth fell open when I saw the spread in front of me – roast beef, lamb chops, fish and chips, Yorkshire pudding, peas, carrots, gravy, ketchup, as well as mint humbugs. As I concentrated on the food, Brandon interrupted my thoughts saying, "the trick is to buy as big a house as is necessary to comfortably accommodate you and your family. Don't forget that your house on mortgage is actually an investment asset of the bank, as it puts money into its pocket in the form of the mortgage installments that you pay to it."

After a high-calorie, but delicious dessert of chocolate brownie with vanilla ice cream, I made myself comfortable in Samuel's room. The Smiths must have been really strict with the interior designer as each nook and corner of the house had been utilized well. I drifted off to sleep with these and other thoughts.

I got up as the first rays of the sun pierced the thin window curtains and lit up my dark room. As I stepped out of the room, I noticed that the Smith home was quiet, yet filled with activity. Lily was busy preparing breakfast, Brandon was cleaning the furniture, while pretty Natasha was reading a book, totally engrossed in it.

"Good morning, John," Brandon said in a loud voice. "How was your night?"

"Pretty good."

"Come, let's have breakfast," Lily said. Just then, the front page headlines of the newspaper lying on the table caught my attention. 'More Casualties of the Subprime Crisis', it read.

"Look at how these guys have been victimized by the subprime crisis. They've lost everything, including the roof over their heads."

"No, my dear friend, they have not been victimized by the subprime crisis, but by their own greed, their need for instant gratification, and their lack of financial wisdom," Brandon philosophized.

As my plate kept being replenished with eggs, bacon, sausage, baked beans and fried bread, he continued, "these folks mistakenly assumed that their house was their biggest asset."

Natasha joined us at the table saying, "bear in mind that every one of your expenses is someone else's income, and each one of your liabilities is someone else's asset.

When you take out a mortgage loan to buy your house, it becomes the investment asset of your bank. The interest which you pay to the bank on your house mortgage becomes income for the bank. Therefore, your expense – interest on your mortgage is the bank's income and your liability – the mortgage loan is the bank's asset," Natasha concluded, biting into her sausages.

Lily added, with great gusto, "it's only because of inflation, which is not really an increase in the value of an asset, but a decline in the value of paper money, that many people feel wealthier as their home's value appears to increase. When they feel wealthier, they borrow more money, that is, negative leverage, and spend more on liabilities, which is a double whammy. This is what is known as the wealth effect. Simply put, it refers to spending that money which you don't have, but imagine as having just on the basis of an increase, or perceived increase, in the price of the asset which you own."

Topping her bread with some eggs and bacon, she continued, "and when the asset price falls, or the value which you thought it commanded does not hold true, you helplessly watch yourself fall into the wealth effect trap. In this trap, you are left with diminished asset prices along with high – cost debt, which your current income is not able to service. For example, a few years ago in the US, home prices kept increasing because of the credit market bubble. Many people borrowed money against their inflated home values. However, when the credit bubble burst, their home was worth much less than what they had borrowed. Those homeowners who were still able to pay their mortgage debt felt terrible as they watched their home prices drop. And those who could not pay their mortgage debt, saw their houses foreclosed and were left only with liabilities and high-cost debt, which they were not able to service. Therefore, always recognize the difference between real and perceived wealth, and never fall into the wealth effect trap."

So engrossed was I in understanding this new concept of the wealth effect trap, that I almost burned my tongue on the hot coffee.

"That is how homeowners end up in the foreclosures office, cutting a sorry figure sans their homes, wealth and self-respect," observed Natasha, who was years ahead of her age as far as financial knowledge was concerned. I wished my daughter was more like Natasha, till I realized I, too, was no Brandon.

"Today, we will be visiting the foreclosures' office," Brandon's strong voice snapped me back to the present. "We will go shopping for good properties there."

This was unusual. Weren't properties snapped up at real estate exhibitions and in the offices of large property developers? Sensing my confusion, Brandon sought to resolve it. "You can buy the best value-for-money property at the foreclosures' office. Just spend a few pounds on its renovation and the value of it almost immediately rises by around 20% as does the potential rent from it. The trick is to buy the right property at the right place at the right price in the right foreclosures auction." He stood up and signaled that it was time to leave.

We were among the early ones to reach the foreclosures' office. We met a number of other bidders, bankers, brokers, and even borrowers. It appeared Brandon was a very familiar face there. And why not? After all, he shopped there regularly for properties.

It was quite a learning experience for me in the foreclosures auction. I saw how the reserve price was fixed, how competitive bidding took place, how the tender forms were filled, and how loans were negotiated. I observed how Brandon bid only on selected properties where he found value, how he let go of houses when the bidding started becoming irrational, and how he doggedly pursued those properties in which he saw scope for improvement and value enhancement. He concluded his deals by talking to his broker about their terms and conditions. He then met his banker and informed him that he would be returning with the necessary documents for a mortgage in a couple of days. After that, he immediately called his office and told them to put out a newspaper advertisement that the house would be available for rent within a month. Everything moved so fast and I marveled at Brandon's supreme confidence in all this.

We stopped for lunch at an Indian restaurant as Brandon was a big fan of Indian cuisine.

"You should always shop in foreclosure auctions when the foreclosed properties are being sold aggressively. Some of the best bargains can be snapped up at such auctions."

Relishing the fresh, Indian *rotis* he continued, "you should also be on the lookout for good distress sale of properties by those facing a cash crunch. *Recession is too important an event, never just let it pass; instead use it to build your wealth. The best of bargains are had at the worst of times.*"

After a sumptuous lunch, we were off to the broker's office for, as Brandon put it, advice on the deal just concluded, as well as any other new, good deals available in the market. Brandon himself appeared to be such an expert on real estate and property, so why would he want the services of a broker and pay unnecessary brokerage, I wondered aloud.

"I saw this question coming. Never underestimate the utility and value of brokers. A good broker can help you find excellent assets at reasonable prices for a small brokerage. Never try to undercut the brokerage. That is his money for the advice he gives you.

However, he cautioned, "when shopping for a broker, don't go for big names because they seldom have the time for you and even if they do, they are rarely in a position to provide you with value, because there could be a number of customers chasing the limited, valuable investment ideas they might have. Instead, try to find someone who is himself a student of investment – a student of his own asset class, a humble learner. This is because money matters and investments are things that nobody in this world can claim to know everything about."

The broker was a person in his mid-30s with around 10 to 12 years of experience. He was very polite and a good listener, besides being a problem solver and someone with a steady stream of ideas. I understood why Brandon had chosen him. He was both a keen learner and an advisor – a true value creator.

Later that day, we were to visit Buckingham Palace, but not before Brandon was all caught up with his office mail.

On our way to Buckingham Palace, Brandon told me that the changing of the guards was a very colorful ceremony, full of royal pageantry. As we entered the palace compound, Brandon pointed to the highest point of the palace and informed me that the presence or absence of the Royal Standard (the royal flag) signaled whether the Queen was or was not in residence.

"Buckingham House was bought in 1761, by George III for his wife, Queen Charlotte, to use as a family home. It is a great tourist attraction. The gardens within Buckingham Palace are said to be home to more than over 350 different types of wildflowers."

Brandon was knowledgeable about the best, as well as cheapest, real estate in town – the properties listed with the foreclosures office.

"When you look at a palace, it's natural to aspire for a big house of one's own, outfitted with all the luxuries. But should you be moving to a bigger house?"

Answering his own question, he said, "home is where one winds down after a hard day's work. It is a place for parents, spouse and children to reside, play and pray. So it's natural for people to own their own house. And everyone wants a big house. However, before deciding to move into a larger house, one should not forget that owning a house entails two types of costs – property tax, maintenance, utility bills and other property-related charges, as also the opportunity cost of the same funds not being utilized for actual investment assets." Catching his breath, he continued, "only after taking into account both these factors, can you decide on the size of house you want to own."

As we toured the palace, Brandon kept up his question and answer session, putting my limited knowledge to constant test.

"This is the royal palace and obviously financed by the government, but tell me, John, who should be financing yours?"

"Obviously me, Brandon. You don't expect me to go begging to somebody else to finance my house?"

Brandon laughed at my outburst, much to my annoyance. "What I meant to ask is, should your house be self-financed or bank-financed? Know that a housing loan offers unique and multiple benefits that probably no other kind of loan offers the highest leverage factor, the cheapest kind of loan with the lowest rate of interest and tax deductions. Notwithstanding the fact that a mortgage is your liability and the bank's asset, as far as possible, you should go for a mortgage and get your house financed by the bank, which will shell out the lion's share of the house cost at the lowest possible rate of interest and then the taxman will grant you all kinds of deductions and exemptions with respect to interest and capital payments.

Just note, John, that it's so funny that the government gives you tax breaks for getting into liabilities and not for buying assets," Brandon smiled.

"And investors chase liabilities to avail these tax deductions," I said.

"Exactly! Once you decide to take out a mortgage, the next issue to settle is whether you should go for fixed or floating interest rates. While buying a mortgage house you are, in effect, dealing with two asset classes at the same time, such as real estate and interest rates."

"So what is the golden rule, Brandon?" I asked eagerly.

Pat came the reply, "you should go in for a floating rate when there has already been a substantial hike in central bank-controlled interest rates over a period of time. On the other hand, you should settle for a fixed rate mortgage loan when there has already been a substantial fall in central bank-controlled interest rates over a period of time.

The next logical question would be when you should buy your house. The best time would be just before the peak in interest rates when the central bank, after raising interest rates several times over the previous months, remains worried about inflation, the banking system liquidity is tight and property prices have cooled down or stabilized. This would, be the best time as you would be buying your dream house at bottom or close to bottom prices, or at that price point after which a reasonable rise in real estate prices commences.

Now let me ask you another question. Who should own your house?"

"Me, of course! After all, it is my own house."

"Yes, it is your own house and most people take pride in owning their own home. But, I regret, that this is not the correct answer, because you are oblivious to corporations and how corporate, tax, securities, property, and succession laws favor a company over an individual."

This discussion was becoming really interesting. Brandon continued, "a corporate structure protects you from many legal financial predators, such as the government, taxman, blackmailers and legal eagles, who use the law to rob you of your possessions, as well as helps with succession planning, which happens automatically with a corporate structure because it has its own separate legal entity with perpetual succession. Whether or not you are alive, the company always survives, unless it is legally wound up by the operation of law.

You have an option of either staying in your own house or renting one. Although it's always emotionally nice to own your own house, but it's financially wise to know the break-even point of your house."

"What on earth is the break-even point of a house?" I was getting impatient now.

Calming me down, Brandon replied, "you have to consider the opportunity cost of money, that is, interest plus the property tax and the other maintenance costs when you buy your house, and then compare it with the rent which you would be paying on a rented house. See which turns out to be cheaper and go in for that option. The point at which they are equal is the break-even point of the house."

He further emphasized that, "your house is a real asset and over the very long-term, notwithstanding fluctuations in the short and medium-term, the value of your house, a real asset, will rise against the artificial thing against which it is measured, that is, paper currency or money."

I felt thrilled to be acquiring such wonderful insights into real estate, standing in front of probably the best and costliest real estate in London – Buckingham Palace. "I get all this in the context of owner-occupied property, but what about rental real estate, Brandon?" I demanded.

"Leave something for tomorrow. Don't try to eat everything in one day."

Changing the mood, he suddenly said, "I was not always this clever about real estate investments. I was crazy about snapping up costly real estate, such as beach houses and holiday homes, and thought nothing about getting deep into debt, convincing myself that real estate prices would always go up. When the subprime crisis burst in 2008, all my real estate prices fell like a pack of cards. My properties were up for foreclosure. It was then that I met Vijay Desai, in one of the foreclosures offices. He not only helped me financially, but also taught me how to be financially savvy. Whatever I have today is because of Vijay. You know, God sends angels like him to this planet to help other mortals like us."

The next morning I was woken up by the sound of hectic activity in the Smith home. Finding Brandon, I said, "hey dude, what's up?"

"Nothing, John, eat your breakfast and get ready quickly, as we are on a mission to see the most beautiful and dangerous sea creatures."

"We are going to the Sea Life London Aquarium, a place with almost 1,000 creatures in more than 2 million liters of water!" Natasha yelled, excitement writ large on her face.

"Indeed," Lily said. "It has 500 species of fish from around the world and 12 species of sharks."

At the aquarium, we started at the shark reef encounter, a glass walkway which allowed us to walk above a stunning shoal of sixteen sharks, including two striking brown sharks, and a group of ten sleek, black-tip reef sharks, as they swam inches below us. Next we came face-to-fin encounters with some awe-inspiring creatures in their magnificent display, spanning three floors and dominated by a selection of imposing Easter Island Heads. The visit concluded with some shark education at the interactive Shark Academy, where everyone got to feel shark skin.

"I hope you enjoyed the adventure? What did you like best?"

"Walking on the sharks was awesome!"

"Imagine what would happen if the glass floor gave way and you fell on to the sharks," Brandon smiled.

"What a morbid thought," I remonstrated.

"But that's what happens to people who invest without knowing, gauging or acknowledging the risks. Always understand the risks and then invest, including in real estate. Yesterday, you asked me about rental real estate, right?"

"Yes, right."

"Don't forget that there is a price risk in rental real estate, as well," Brandon cautioned me. "But that should not worry you, because I am not asking you to buy real estate in expectation of an increase in its value, so that you can flip it at a higher price for capital gains. That is never the right premise to buy any asset, including real estate.

Invest in real estate for earning income and aim to make it net positive cash flow after tax. Once you follow this principle, you need not worry about the price of your property."

Lily joined the conversation to say, "don't forget, the cardinal principle of investment is that, if you are investing for passive income, then capital gains would invariably follow. The reason is very simple. When you invest for income and evaluate the investment proposal, you will look at the potential passive return in the form of dividend yield for a stock, bond yield on maturity of a bond, and rental yield for real estate. Then you will strive for net cash flow positive after tax, which might not be possible in many cases, but the point is that once you start thinking along these lines, you will naturally go for reasonably valued assets, because only value gives higher yield.

Always bear in mind that money is made in investments not at the time of selling, but at the time of buying. If your entry point for any investment asset is reasonably right, you will eventually make money. Thus, money is made at the point of buying, but only realized at the time of selling. In fact, in a housing market crash, many homes will be put up for foreclosure and this will raise the demand for rental house and push up rents."

It was evening when we headed back. The streets and pavements of London were choked with cars and pedestrians. I noticed Brandon was busy checking emails on his cellphone.

"There is some water leakage in one of my rental properties. The tenants want immediate action."

"This is the problem with rental real estate. That's why I prefer to steer clear of it."

"If a subject is difficult should the student ignore it or try to find a way to resolve it? If the economy is not performing well, should policy makers wash their hands of it or be proactive? Why, if your patient contracts some deadly disease, do you try to cure him or leave him to die?" Brandon was becoming agitated.

"I will, of course, try to cure the patient to the best of my ability."

"So then why do you expect to succeed without problems or win without losing? Just because there are some problems, you don't abandon the opportunity, do you?"

Taking over from her husband, Lily interjected, "the resolution of all property-related issues, such as leakages, painting of the walls and ceilings, water issues, security problems, even the collection of rent, is best left to professionals called property managers. Just hire them."

"Yes, that's the perfect arrangement," echoed Brandon.

I got the message – no one should abandon his goals in life simply because the path to it is full of thorns.

That evening, we ordered in pizza and shared tales from our lives with one another. Before retiring for the night, Brandon told me to sleep well, so I was well prepared for the next day's 'horrors', refusing to divulge more than that.

The gnawing anxiety of what the day was to bring must have played on my mind, as I was up at 4 am and could not sleep a wink thereafter.

What had Brandon meant by horrors? Was it something related to money? Was it something to do with Vijay Desai? Was it something linked to my extraordinary journey? Oh, what was it?

I jumped out of bed; it was very quiet and dark outside. I knew my anxiety would only worsen if I sat still, so I decided to freshen up and get ready for the day. I tried to focus on the financial lessons I had learned these past few days, hoping the positive thoughts would keep my nerves in check. In any case, the past 22 days had brought to life the horrors of my past financial life. Soon, I noticed the first signs of daybreak.

After a good breakfast, we left on our so-called journey of horror. The car sped on the empty morning roads, as we headed straight toward London Bridge. Was this the place that was going to give me a horror-filled experience?

"See, hear, feel, taste, even smell, what London Bridge was like over the ages," Brandon said.

We first watched the thrilling show of late Queen Boudicca's battle with the Romans in AD 60. It was full of surprises that punctuated the darkness and caused everyone to jump. Natasha whispered to me, "continue your adventure with caution, as you will now cross the cavernous infinity floor in the thick fog and perilous setting of the Viking king, Olaf's, rule as he pulls London Bridge down in 1012." I had to really watch my step on the rickety wooden bridge and it was a really long way down.

Then it was time to enter the Gate House and discover the grisly fate of the Tudor Traitors. I also noticed two giant Gambian pouched rats. I learned about the trades that were common in the 1600s, and then ran down the burning bridge to escape the great fire of 1666.

"Just as you ran down the bridge to escape the fire, you have to take proper care of your house to prevent it from catching fire," Brandon yelled at me in the commotion. I nodded my head and wondered if what I was being put through was physical, mental, psychological or spiritual training – whatever it was, it was great. What I did not know then, was that the best was yet to come.

I got a taste of medieval life as I passed through the Chapel of Thomas Becket and onto the shop-lined streets of the old London Bridge. There were darker surprises in store for us as we traversed the streets of Victorian Southwark. I caught a whiff of the 'Great Stink' and was clever enough to not become another victim of Jack the Ripper. My fiery journey ended with Hell's Portal.

"How did you find the Hollywood-style wizardry?" Brandon asked. "Did you have fun while also learning a bit about London's gruesome history?"

"Yeah," I said, trying to catch my breath.

"It's a thrilling experience. The latest in Hollywood style wizardry and some marvelous real life characters through the ages leaves us entertained as well as amazed at what we see," observed the witty teen Natasha.

"Now I will take you on a tour of London city. And, unlike the London Bridge tour, where we had to pay money, we will earn money from the London city tour!"

Brandon must think I have lost my mind to believe this drivel! I glared at him as Lily stepped in to clarify. "What Brandon means is that we will collect the rent owed to us from our tenants and managers as we go around the city."

I got to see up close how Brandon dealt with his tenants, property managers and brokers. Even as Brandon took his tenants' complaints in stride, he also kept a sharp eye for how he could add value to the property, so as to be able to increase the rent.

"Brandon, do you think your house value will appreciate?"

"I don't know whether my particular house price will go up, but overall, real estate will appreciate over the long-term, notwithstanding short-to medium-term fluctuations.

Over the very long term, the price of real estate always tends to go up because of two factors. First, the aggregate supply of real estate is limited, while the supply of money against which it is measured, is practically unlimited as governments can, and do, print money whenever they want. Second, because of inflation, the replacement cost of the house or, in other words, the construction cost, increases. For example, the price of cement, steel, labor, etc., keeps rising and, therefore, the price of the house has to rise commensurately for the developer to make money on it."

I always speculated on whether the price of my house would increase, but never had the common sense to see it the way Brandon had explained. Common sense is, indeed, very uncommon.

"That means the price of my house will always increase over the long-term," I said, excitedly.

"Now that will depend on several factors, including development in your locality, improvements made to your house, and economic activity in the vicinity of your house. 'Location, location, location,' is the refrain I constantly hear in the context of real estate purchases. However, I beg to differ. I believe the most important factors affecting the price of your house are the changes occurring in your locality. Say you buy a house in the best of localities, its price would have taken into account all the locational advantages offered by it. So the future price of your house will increase only if there is some incremental development there in the form of, say, a new school, a hospital, a railway station, shopping mall, or even new job opportunities."

As he got busy with yet another email on his cellphone, Lily continued the thread. "Improvements to the house itself, such as a new coat of paint, the installation of air conditioners or heaters, electric lights and fittings, geyser, etc., can also certainly increase the value of the house."

Finishing his email, Brandon took over. "There are also some general factors that affect the price of real estate, the main among them being economic growth. This leaves people with more money to spend on their houses, and interest rates. The lower the interest rates, the higher the demand for homes and thereore, the tendency of prices to hold firm."

Lily added, "other factors affecting home prices would be government policies, legislation and subsidies, development of the banking system and availability of credit." She removed a dark red lipstick from her handbag and began applying it.

Just then a distinctive ring came through Brandon's cell phone. "Oh, that's my brother," Natasha exclaimed.

"Hey dude, how are you doing," shouted Brandon on his cell. After chatting for a couple of minutes with his son, he handed over the phone to his wife, who hastily put away the lipstick to chat with her son. Soon, Natasha snatched the handset from her mom to hear her brother's voice. My eyes became moist as I remembered my wife and children. It was more than three weeks since I had seen or even talked to them.

"Here Mr John, my brother, Samuel, would like to speak with you," Natasha extended the phone toward me.

A strong, young voice said, "good afternoon, Mr John, I am sure you are enjoying your stay in London in the company of my family. I want to add my share of knowledge on real estate. Governments generally give tax incentives to buy liabilities. So never buy a house or, for that matter, any asset just to avail tax deductions. The asset should make economic sense. Always buy real estate which generates net positive cash flow after tax." Saying this, he bid me goodbye and hung up.

That evening, I decided to spend some time alone trawling the streets of London. As my mind went over everything I had learned thus far, I wondered what my friend, Vijay Desai's, letter would contain this time.

After dinner, Brandon came to my room and handed over an envelope and a small memento that carried the picture of a temple. I did not understand its significance and carefully proceeded to open it.

Recognizing the Real Value of Real Estate

Just as God showers wealth on His devotees, so must the real estate you own put money into your pocket.

Your house is like a temple which you should aim to own for self occupation, keeping in mind the hard truth that it is a bad capital asset purchased to save on the unnecessary revenue expenditure in the form of rent. Don't forget the eternal truth that your house is not your investment asset but that of the bank simply because it puts your money into the banker's pocket in the form of mortgage loan instalments. Since a house has the highest leverage factor, and mortgage is generally the cheapest form of bank credit and one on which the taxman gives the most deductions and exemptions, it makes sense to fund your house through a mortgage loan from the bank. Depending on the interest rate cycle, choose the correct type of interest rate, fixed or floating. Try to buy your house just before the peak in interest rates – when property prices would have come down. A house owned by your company protects it from legal financial predators, including the government and the taxman, as well as aids in proper succession planning. Opportunity has a queer way of stalking the person who can recognize it and is ready to embrace it. Panic creates opportunity as 'one man's loss is another man's profit.' Recession is too important an event, never just let it pass, instead use it to build your wealth. Shopping at the foreclosures office or buying from distressed sellers can get you a clear bargain price. Never undermine the usefulness of good brokers and property managers – they are your true partners in successful real estate investments. Reward them with their share of fair remuneration and they will present you with more than your share of profitable investment opportunities. *Never try to demand more than you deserve from this world and this includes your real estate.* If you attempt to extract equity from your house based on its unrealized, expected value then you are sure to fall prey to the wealth effect. Real estate is a big emotional investment that requires investment skill as well as mental balance – don't quit when the going is hard. *Aim to make rental real estate with positive net cash flow after tax one of your investment assets because that will put hard cash into your pocket, in perpetuity.*

What is Protected is What is Kept

The next morning, I was ready to move to my next destination. The clock had turned full circle, I was returning to India. Yes, I was flying back to Mumbai. As I waited to check in at the London airport, a cup of hot cappuccino in hand, my mind wandered to all the places I had travelled to, and the incredible people I had met and interacted with over the past 23 days.

I boarded the flight with mixed feelings – happy to be returning to my country, but at the same time, sorry for parting from such unbelievable teachers. However, one thing was certain, I was returning home a cleverer, wiser and more inspired person. I was returning to my country, but I was soon to discover that my journey was not yet quite over.

When I came out of the airport, it was 3.30 am in Mumbai – call it late night or early morning. I noticed a

neatly dressed short man with a French beard waiting outside
the gate with a signboard carrying my name. I waved at him
and he hurried up to me to help with my luggage to the car
park. As I settled back in the car, he informed me that he was
the driver of my next mentor. It turned out we were heading
to Deolali, a small village near Nashik, about 180 kilometers
north of Mumbai. His manner and bearing suggested a
military connection, and my suspicions were confirmed when
he revealed he was a former military driver, now working for
Captain Shyam Singh.

As the car sped through the empty roads of Mumbai in
the wee hours, I speculated about my next teacher. Would
he fit the stereotype of a dour military man? Would he be
approachable? What could a military man have to teach me
about money?

I have no idea when I dozed off, but when I woke up,
we were driving up a mountain, the Kasara ghat. I watched
the first rays of sun filtering through the darkness. A thick fog
hung over the area as we reached the highest point on the
plateau – Igatpuri. After another drive of about 45 minutes,
our car went past military vehicles and entered some kind of
restricted area, where civilians are not allowed, and halted in
front of a small house. The driver leapt out and carried my
luggage indoors. As I stood outside breathing in the fresh air,
a polite voice said, "welcome to my cottage."

The first thing I noticed as I entered the cottage was its
brightly painted walls. Beautiful lamps lined one side of the
living room and colorful paintings stared down from the walls.
The Indian furniture showed the owner's exquisite taste. I was
so lost in my surroundings that I almost missed a voice saying,
"welcome home, my friend," till it was very close.

Oh God! What was this? The voice was coming from a man in a wheelchair!

He was wearing a simple, but ironed shirt, and his legs were covered with a big blanket. He appeared to be in his mid-40s.

"Welcome to Deolali! I am Captain Shyam Singh and the one chosen to pass on the last nugget of wisdom in your soul-searching journey around the world for financial knowledge," he said, extending his hand. "But before we talk finance, I want you to relax. Come, let's have tea and some mouth-watering local breakfast."

My senses came alive the moment I took my first sip of the hot tea, brewed with fresh mint and chai masala. The *aloo* and *methi* paratha with curd, as well as the butter and jam with hard bakery bread, was just the kind of food I craved since leaving home three weeks earlier. Catching my furtive glances at his wheelchair and, perhaps, sensing my pity, the captain said, "I may be a slave of this wheelchair, but I am not the slave of money. It is very unfortunate that even as we are advancing technologically, we are regressing financially and becoming slaves of money.

The problem with today's youth is that although they earn handsomely, they spend more than they earn, are not able to protect themselves from financial predators, buy liabilities with negative leverage believing it to be assets, fall into a debt trap and so, become slaves to money for life. I am very pained to see this and this is why I decided to share my financial sagacity with seekers like you."

"That is really nice of you," I said quietly noticing both passion and pain in his shining eyes.

"I'm sure you are curious to know my story, so here it is. I was a captain in the Indian Army and was seen as highly intelligent and a strong personality. I was the pride of my cantonment. I was often held up as a role model for the *jawans*. I had once heard a Swami say, 'to live to hundred, you need not be alive for hundred years, but do such great work in one day that people will remember you for the next hundred years'. I took this to heart.

You must have heard about the Kargil War. I lost my legs to a bomb explosion, while protecting my post and fellow soldiers."

Just then a strong gust of wind rattled the windows, blowing off his blanket and revealing his leg stumps. I felt so overwhelmed that I instinctively got up and saluted this true war hero. He smiled and continued, "just as I was not able to protect my leg from the enemy, I was also unable to protect myself from love and money predators."

Now what did he mean by love and money predators?

"I once loved a beautiful girl, whose affections for me increased in direct proportion to the increase in my wealth. When I lost my legs, job and wealth, I also lost her love. Rather, I should say, God saved me from her, a dangerous love predator," he said, clearly agitated.

"I had to quit the army. However, I did get pension, as well as this house from the government, but I lost most of my money to the legal financial predators."

Who are these legal financial predators? "There are different legal financial predators – legal – because they take money from your pocket legally at different stages of your monetary transactions."

Captain Singh told me he met Vijay at one of the Army Day celebrations, where Vijay had been invited as a guest speaker. It was Vijay who put him on the road to financial freedom.

Later that day, we drove around the army cantonment in the vicinity of the captain's house. I saw arms and ammunition being transported in military trucks. Suddenly, gunshots rang out in the distance. "The artillery training center is just behind that hill," the captain explained, pointing to the other side of the road.

"You must be very familiar with scenes of jostling crowds on Mumbai's local trains, as people head to work."

I nodded my head vigorously.

"But do you know that these people take this painful journey for four out of 12 months for the government?"

I raised my eyebrows.

"The government collects income tax and this is no small amount. It is almost a third of the income for people falling in the highest tax bracket. So, roughly a third of a person's working life is devoted to working for the government."

I marveled at this very novel way of looking at taxes.

Captain Singh continued, "but taxes are necessary for the government for nation-building, infrastructure, construction, education, housing, welfare schemes, and, of course, the defense of our mighty nation. Even my pension comes from this tax money."

"So then, there is no way to protect oneself from the taxman," I said, worried.

"Of course, there is. Do what the government wants you to do and it will let you save tax – legally. The government does not want you to work for money. It actually wants your money to work for you. So, don't go for work all squashed up in crowded trains, rather send your money to work for you," he smiled, mysteriously.

"Make your money work for you through investment assets generating tax-free returns. For example, if you invest in equities, the dividend on that is tax-free, while long-term capital gains are exempt from capital gains taxation. Similarly, if you start some business in a place where the government wants you to put up a plant, it will grant you a tax holiday for many years. In the army, we listen to what the government is saying. Similarly, while dealing with your money, you should listen to what the government is saying and save yourself some tax – legally."

We then went to a bank. I noticed the captain take out his chequebook, write out a cheque and hand it to the bank clerk. As we waited for the clerk to process it, my mentor said, "this was the monthly EMI on the car which I had purchased for the so-called love of my life with a bank loan. Now that the car is gone with the love predator, I am saddled with this bank loan." His face clearly depicted the pain of betrayal.

Collecting his receipt, he said, "this is what happens when we buy liabilities, believing them to be assets, out of borrowed money. The EMI amount may appear to be small, but it ensures you remain lifelong slaves. Once one EMI is settled, you will be sucked into buying another product on another so-called low EMI. The cycle is never-ending, the slavery is permanent."

We returned home and tucked into a typical Punjabi lunch of naan and roti, paneer, sabzi, dal, rice, pickle and more, topped off with thick, delicious, sweet lassi. After such a heavy lunch, I just had to take a long nap.

In the evening, I joined the captain to go to a downtown mall. At many of the large retail outlets, I saw the customers lured into subscribing to their retail credit cards with a promise of reward points.

"These are not reward points, but punishment points. Once you fall into their trap, they will make you buy all kinds of unwanted items on credit. For a small redemption amount of say, ₹100, they will lure you into buying goods worth ₹1,000. It's a vicious cycle as these parasitic corporate retailers will keep going after your money. They will keep making you buy the things you don't need with the result that very soon you will be forced to sell the things you do need."

Once we were done with shopping, we stopped briefly at a coffee shop, before heading back home. After dinner, I had an emotional telephone conversation with my family, for the very first time, since embarking on this long journey. Soon, my body caved and I was snoring the moment my head hit the pillow.

I was up early, as usual. I must say, the morning was very pleasant in this village of Deolali – the sunrise, the birds chirping, the dogs playing and the cows being milked. I felt like I was returning to my roots, like being re-introduced to my inner self.

Captain Singh had said we would be visiting some of Nashik's famous vineyards. On the way, we stopped at a pharmacy to buy his medicines. Nodding toward a young woman buying an expensive cosmetic item, the captain smiled.

"These cosmetics may or may not make women look beautiful, but they certainly add to the health of the government."

Catching my confused look, he explained, "while income tax is a direct tax on the person who is earning it and so, easily recognizable, there is a bigger menace that systematically eats into your wealth without you even knowing it. And that is the indirect tax like excise, customs, service tax, etc. These, levied on the goods and services that you buy, can range from anywhere between 4% and 30%. Of the ₹100 paid for the cosmetic item, around ₹30 goes to the government in the form of these indirect taxes and duties."

I thought of all the times I had dined at expensive restaurants, bought luxury items, and availed myself of fancy services, without realizing how much of it was going into government coffers.

Very soon, we were in one of the most famous vineyards of Nashik. It was exhilarating to see how the grapes were pressed in large, turbine-like machines. We even picked up a few bottles of the fresh, strong wine.

While returning from the vineyard, Captain Singh said, "that wine tasted so heavenly, because it has been stored well and allowed to ferment. The same way, if you invest your money for the long-term, using the *right vehicle*, you will be able to protect it from financial predators. You will be able to preserve and grow your wealth."

I asked him to explain what he meant by 'right vehicle'.

"Your income-earning vehicle simply means the type of legal entity from which you earn your income. There are basically two kinds of vehicles through which you can earn money – individual and corporate. There are distinct advantages, for earning, investing and holding, of an institutional structure over an individual."

"Can you elaborate on this," I requested.

"Sure. The most important advantage of the corporate structure over an individual is related to taxes. The tax laws are regressive and discriminatory – they punish the hard working person, who earns money through his labor and rewards the person, who relaxes and lets his money work for him. This discrimination is even more glaring at the time of earning money, if you are not using the right vehicle to earn it. The person earning guaranteed, passive, or portfolio income has the choice of either using the individual or the institutional vehicle."

"But what is the advantage of the institutional vehicle?"

"The advantage is that as an individual, you first pay tax to the government before meeting your expenses. But for an institution, you first pay all the expenses out of the pre-tax money and then pay taxes, if any, to the government." On our way back home, we visited the Trimbakeshwar Shiv Temple, the Someshwar Temple, and the Sitimata Cave. It was a tiring day, but very fulfilling, not only because of what I got to see, but also because of what I had learned.

The next day was pleasant and sunny. After a typical heavy Indian breakfast, we took another tour of the cantonment. We visited the army school and interacted with the children, returning to the captain's cottage for lunch.

"Have you ever invested in a mutual fund," came a seemingly random question from my mentor.

"Yes."

"Tell me which is the best fund for investment?"

My mind began to work furiously to decide, but before I could answer, Captain Singh answered his own question. "The balance fund. The name is actually misleading, because this fund is tilted heavily in favor of the investor by protecting and shielding his money from all five investment thieves, which include inflation, income tax, interest rates, market volatility and incorrect asset allocation. So the next time you see a balance fund, don't just brush it aside. Remember, whether dealing with investments or life, a simple and balanced approach always works."

With these words, he handed over an envelope, which came with a small memento of a 'soldier', and quietly turned around his wheelchair back to his room.

Shield Yourself from Predators

Just as a soldier stands guard outside a fort, so must you guard your life and wealth from predators who legally and systematically rob you of your money, happiness and life.

Learn how to deal with money predators, such as the government, bankers, brokers, retailers etc., both at the time of earning money and while picking the vehicle (individual or institutional) through which you earn money. You can save substantial amounts of money by earning it in the right category – earned income, guaranteed income, passive income and portfolio income. The way the taxman treats different categories is very different and *you should know how to convert your earned income into passive and portfolio income so as to pay the minimum to, or altogether avoid, the taxman.* As an individual, you incur all expenses on post-tax money while as an institution all expenses are incurred on pre-tax money. Thus, *as an individual you first pay tax to the government, while as an institution you first pay yourself and then to the government via taxes from the money left, if any.* Increase your financial and legal literacy by studying accountancy, corporate, taxation and securities laws so as to make the right choice of the earning, investing, holding and succession planning vehicle.

The Most Important Lesson

I left Nashik with a heavy heart, greatly moved by the sacrifice of a fellow countryman. Captain Shyam Singh was a man who had fought not only against a physical enemy, but also against financial slavery. I was on my way back to Mumbai from Deolali, but was told my next destination would be somewhere in the Himalayas, where I would receive the most important lesson of my life. As the car sped on to the Nashik–Mumbai highway, all kinds of thoughts ran through my mind. I had already received all the ten nuggets of financial wisdom, so what great lesson awaited me in the mighty Himalayas and who would be my next guru? I reached Mumbai airport late evening to catch the night flight. As I waited to check in, the irony of the fact that I was physically so close to my family and yet could not see them, hit me.

When I landed in Delhi, it was 11 pm. A car was waiting for me. I was informed by the driver that we were headed toward the holy town of Haridwar. We would reach early morning, he said. As I gazed out of the window, I was struck by the numerous billboards and their glossy images of a handsome boy in a cowboy hat smoking a cigarette, two beautiful young women smiling over a shampoo bottle, a sultry-looking teenager with her jeans half-zipped, a sexy woman in a black velvet dress, and a man in a tuxedo, snuggling over a cup of coffee. Soon, I fell asleep.

I woke up to a vigorous shaking by the driver. We had reached Haridwar in the wee hours. We went to a local restaurant for some tea and breakfast. Then he took me to the Ganges for a purifying dip, as though to wash away all my financial sins. After crossing a section of the river on the *Rishikeshjhula*, an iron suspension bridge, we commenced our journey toward Gangotri. I had read that it is located more than 10,000 feet above sea level. Gangotri, the origin of the River Ganges and seat of the Goddess Ganga, is one of the four sites of the *Char Dham* pilgrimage circuit. The origin of the holy river is Gaumukh, set in the Gangotri Glacier, and is a 19 kilometer trek from Gangotri. We left Haridwar at around 10.30 am and reached Gangotri at 4 pm, having halted half an hour for lunch. Although I love mountain trekking and knew about Gangotri and the *Char Dham*, I had never found the time to visit any of them, since I was busy earning money. *Being enslaved by money left me with no time to pursue my hobbies.*

"You have reached your destination, sir," smiled the driver. "You are now ready to learn the eternal truth, which you have forgotten in your money chase," he said, before thrusting a piece of paper in my hands and disappearing into the mountain roads.

When I opened the piece of paper, it said, 'the enlightened one is waiting for you at Gangotri Ashram. Go face the eternal truth of money, wealth, life and beyond.'

I went to a nearby tea stall for directions to the ashram. "You are lucky, my friend, to have this opportunity to know the divine truth and end all your problems, money wise and otherwise."

I could hardly wait to reach the ashram. When I got there, I was greeted with, "welcome to Swamiji's palace. The place where you live, love and worship is no less sacred than a temple and no less beautiful than a palace."

Slowly and dramatically, the person behind the voice appeared in front of me. I had never seen anyone with a more magnetic personality. He exuded such immense power. Although in his late 60s, he looked youthful, with a head full of white hair and in superb physical condition. And his eyes! I will never forget those eyes. They were the most piercing and remarkable eyes I had ever seen.

"You will not get financial wisdom from me. But you will get such wisdom as will open your mind to finance," he said.

"But who are you?" I asked, respectfully.

"Really, nobody, but people call me Swami Sidheshwara."

"Are you some kind of divine power?"

"Everything that has name and form must begin in time, exist in time and end in time," he said, mysteriously. "Everything that occupies space has form. The forms have value only in the sense of being expressions of the life within. The forms are evanescent, but the spirit, being in the Lord and of the Lord, is immortal and omnipresent. Everything that has name and form is transient and must die. That is why God has no form."

I was dumbfounded. Here was a truly enlightened soul. I felt privileged to be standing in front of him.

Just then, a woman came in with a tray of tea and snacks. Swamiji accepted it gracefully and blessed her. "Come, join me. Whatever I need comes to me. The time and energy I invested in the betterment and enlightenment of mankind is now coming back to me in the form of food, clothing and other necessities. The same way, if you invest your time and money in investment assets, the income from it will flow to you for life."

Oh my God! I could not believe this. Swamiji was combining spiritual and material wealth with such ease.

"And once one's investment assets start working and generating income, financial freedom is achieved, right?"

"In a sense, yes, but true financial freedom will come only when you are free physically, mentally and spiritually. Freedom is the goal of nature, sentient and insentient. Consciously or unconsciously, every struggle is aimed at reaching that goal. One seeks neither misery nor happiness, pleasure nor sorrow, life nor death. What one seeks is freedom. Although man is essentially free, he will have to discover it. The wisdom you have gained over the past four weeks will set you free, money wise and otherwise.

"Now you tell me, do you have to attain financial freedom to have money?"

"I don't think so," I said, haltingly.

"Money cannot give you freedom. It can only make you it slave. So be the master of money; don't ever be afraid of it and never run after it. Money is not the solution to our problems, financial knowledge is," Swamiji said, gulping his tea.

"Money cannot give you either name or fame. Hold your money merely as custodian for what is God's. Money is not evil when it is in good hands," he continued, as he stood up to leave for his prayer session, leaving me to enjoy my heavenly surroundings.

I found myself having a rather early dinner, by 7 pm, which I told was the norm in the mountains. As always, the food came from one of Swamiji's devotees, who delivered it with great love and respect. Like Swamiji said, carefully bought assets will always reward one with constant income.

When I woke up the next morning, I felt extremely refreshed. I had the most restful sleep of my life. It felt as if that night my soul had been to heaven and back!

Swamiji was in prayer when I joined him.

"Prayer has no meaning, unless you offer it sincerely from your heart. God will never accept your prayers, unless you love and respect all his creations," he said.

As we settled down for breakfast, I asked Swamiji, "how would you describe sickness and ageing?"

"It's not sickness and the ageing of the body that you should fear, rather be afraid of the ageing of the mind and the sickness of the soul."

"What about negative thoughts, feelings and emotions like fear, doubt, pride, jealousy, anxiety, etc?"

"Thoughts are things. Life's battles aren't always won by the one who is stronger or faster, but by the person who perseveres in times of failure. That which you think today becomes that which you are tomorrow.

And what are these negative feelings and emotions, anyway? Nothing but manifestations of one's own mind. Never fear taking risks in life. Remaining in one's comfort zone is the biggest risk of all, since it's the most dangerous and uncertain zone on this planet. The fears you run from actually run toward you, so never be fearful. And, remember, every time you actually do what you fear, you take back the power that fear has stolen from you and reclaim the unclaimed strength within you. In the money world, too, fear can be one's big enemy. For example, the fear of losing money may not allow you to invest in equities. Consequently, your money will lie idle in your bank, constantly being eaten up by the monsters of taxation and inflation."

"What if one is always in doubt?"

"Doubt forces you into wrong decisions and sometimes even paralyzes your decision-making, which can be very detrimental to you, financially and otherwise."

"But some people are habitual worriers."

"Correct! Some people worry constantly. Even if there is no problem, they worry so much that eventually they create some problem. Because of their anxiety, they are not able to enjoy the small and beautiful experiences of life."

"What about pride and ego?"

"They are two of mankind's most formidable enemies. Pride leads to downfall, whether in one's personal, professional, spiritual or investment lives. And ego is worse than pride, as it can cloud your vision while dealing with anything in life, including money."

"And jealousy?"

"Jealousy creates a cloud of discontent, resentment, anger and frustration around you, which mars your vision and puts you at substantial risk of taking the wrong decisions, including poor financial one."

"There are also those who pity themselves."

"Ah, yes!" he exclaimed. "Never pity yourself. Whatever is happening in your life, good or bad, is happening for a purpose and is the result of many factors, some known, others unknown, like your karma. So if you think you are being punished, it is because of your own deeds. At the same time, don't feel embarrassed when you are rewarded. Be humble, but enjoy the reward, because you deserve it.

It is common sense that not respecting the most precious thing you have is a big mistake, but it is not easy to know what is most precious to you. Some may think it's money, fame or power, or the like. But actually, your most precious asset is the one you have an uninterrupted supply of, but it is non-renewable. Once you lose it, you never ever get it back again and that is time. Yes, my friend, time is the most precious asset in this world and when you lose it, even with all the wealth in the world, you can never get it. So you must have the discipline to focus your time on your priorities. Plan your time properly, because failing to plan is, in fact, planning to fail. Every time you say yes to something that is unimportant, you are unknowingly saying no to something that is important. Guard your time well, as it will help you generate money and happiness.

There are some qualities you must cultivate to lead an enriched and successful life. One is belief; if you believe you can do something, you will be able do it, but if you believe you cannot do something, then you cannot do it. In both cases, you are right. Another is humility; if you are humble, many of your enemies, such as pride, ego, jealousy, etc. will automatically vanish. Then, there is patience, persistence and hard work which are the essential ingredients for success. Don't forget the importance of character. Reputation is that which people think you are, your character is that which you actually are. Have a positive attitude as your attitude determines how high you go. Also, never underestimate the power of questioning; ask and the world will give, because everybody is trained from childhood to give what is asked for."

Even as I tried to absorb all these wonderful ideas, he continued, "never be afraid of taking risks. In fact, always take calculated risks. Whether you know it or not, you are continuously being subjected to different kinds of risk. For example, to love exposes you to the risk of it not being reciprocated; to laugh is to run the risk of being seen as a fool; to weep is to appear sloppy and the biggest risk of all, is to live because to live is to risk dying. We have to constantly take some kind of risk or other to learn, grow and win.

Nothing in this world has the power to hold you back other than your own self," he said, before getting up to meet his disciples, who had gathered outside. I observed the love and dignity with which he greeted, met, spoke, advised, and treated his devotees.

I felt like I was in a divine presence.

I continued to bombard Swamiji with my inexhaustible questions over lunch, which, of course, had been prepared by some of his disciples.

"What are your thoughts on marriage?"

"You are asking this of someone who is celibate," Swamiji laughed. "Almost everyone I know has had a problem with marriage. Some had problems getting into it, some getting out of it. The problem with today's youth is that they are either too selfish or have no time to nurture a loving relationship. They don't know what they want in their partner. In fact, they don't even know themselves, so how can they know their marriage partner?

There are a few rules I know to be true about love and marriage – if you don't respect the other person, you are going to have a lot of trouble. If you don't know how to compromise, you are inviting trouble. If you can't talk openly about what is going on between the two of you, you are sure to get into trouble. And if you don't have a common set of values in life, you will suffer much heartache. Your thinking may be different, but your values must match."

How true! I had often quarreled with my wife and a lot of this was because I did not respect her feelings, understand her, appreciate what she was doing, I did not compromise, and I did not speak to her, but at a deeper level, our values did match and that is why our marriage had survived.

"What are your views on work?"

"Everyone has some talents that they want to express. And the way they do this is by engaging in activities they enjoy, be it gardening, cleaning, sweeping, farming, cooking, raising children, even praying. Don't confuse work with just earning money. Any healthy activity which adds value to you or the world around is work. On the other hand, those who work for the sake of earning money, are just spending their time. Such people are not actually working, but hiding behind their work, hiding from others, from their families, their superiors, and colleagues and above all, from their own souls. *They don't have the courage to live their own dreams and that is why they hide behind their work.* They seldom attain freedom, money wise and otherwise.

When people, in pursuit of material gains overlook the very reason of their existence, they live a very empty life, being disconnected from the universe and their inner self."

This explained why so many people appear so busy and work all day. They are, as Swamiji said, avoiding the world, escaping from other people, giving in to their fears, living a big lie and above all, not fulfilling the duty of their soul.

"What are your views on success and failure?"

"Failure does not mean you were unable to complete a task, but just that you did not give your best to your task. Success does not mean winning every battle, but it means winning the final war. Failure means moving from initial defeat to final victory. One should learn to brace oneself for failure, rather than success, because failure is far more common than success. Remember that we learn the most from our failures. When life sends you one of its challenges, it actually helps crack you open so that all the love, power and potential that had been sleeping inside you can pour forth. Initial failure is the stepping stone to ultimate success.

And remember," he added prophetically. "I would fear two kinds of people – the one who has never failed and the one who repeats the same mistake more than once, which leads to his failure, since these are the people who have either never done anything worthwhile in their lives, or not learned from their failures."

Pausing for a moment, he said with a mischievous smile, "and speaking of success, I don't know too many people in this world who understand success. Failure is a very good teacher, while success is a very bad master. You can fail and then succeed, but if you don't know how to handle success, then you could end up worse than a failure. Don't forget that nothing fails like success, because when you are at the top, it's so easy to stop doing the very things that took you there."

There was no questioning that last bit. My own life was example of the fact that it was so easy to forget the very principles that made one rich, like protecting, budgeting, leveraging, investing, insuring, when one is at the top of the wealth cycle.

"What do you think can be man's biggest regret while dealing with money?" I asked.

"To earn without protecting, to spend without budgeting, to save without investing, to invest without learning, to grow money without leveraging, to work without insuring, to die without living," came the instant response, before Swamiji disappeared indoors for his prayers.

The evening passed quietly in the tranquil environs of the majestic mountains. The next day would be the penultimate day of my incredible journey. But rather than my journey ending, I felt like I was on the threshold of a new beginning.

Over tea the next morning, I continued to grill my mentor.

"Swamiji, you have said that everything that has form must perish. So what is your view on life and death?"

"The soul is eternal and immortal, perfect and infinite, it is beyond life and death. When the body dies, the soul takes on a new body. Death is like life's shadow, it follows man everywhere. Life is like one's teacher, and death only makes it possible to begin all over again.

To live to hundred, one need not be alive for hundred years. In one day, do such work that people will remember you for the next hundred years," he said, repeating what I had heard from my previous mentor, Captain Shyam Singh. I now realized he had heard it from none other than Swami Sidheshwara.

"Don't fear death, fear the loss of your life," he continued. "Most of the people lack the courage to follow their convictions. They dress like others, think like others, and behave like others, even if doing so does not seem right to them. They surrender to the known, rather than exploring the unknown, even though their heart tells them otherwise. Death is just one more way of losing your life.

Don't fear that life will end one day, rather feel threatened by the fact that it may never begin," continued Swamiji as he swallowed his tea. "It's better to quit while you are at your peak, rather than wait to decay. Connect with your death as the human form is ultimately going to end to give way to the spiritual one. We are all spiritual beings having a human experience.

And death can take many forms. Paralysis of the body is physical death; a non-performing mind is mental death; an ugly soul is spiritual death – so don't blame death for anything, rather blame the life that you did not live. Therefore, strive to achieve greatness while you are still alive One must never forget one's 'true calling' because this is a pact we make with God before embarking on our earthly journey. The 'true calling' is in reality a personal calling that acts like a trigger in our soul, telling us who we are and what our purpose is in life. To be able to identify and follow that call is clearly our mission on earth – the reason for our very existence.

And always bear in mind that to give short-term happiness to your temporary physical body, never do long-term damage to your permanent soul."

Saying this, Swamiji removed a sealed envelope from his rucksack and handed it to me. "This is the final letter from your friend, Vijay Desai. It was his last wish that you read this letter when you reach your home."

He then walked away into the far horizons. I spent the whole day alone in Swamiji's house and left for Mumbai that evening. But one thing that Swamiji had said kept troubling me.

What did he mean by it being Vijay's last wish for me to read his letter?

The Final Letter

After spending a quiet day alone in the serene Himalayan mountains, I embarked on the long journey back home. I reached Delhi Airport in the early hours of the 30th day of my journey around the world, seeking financial wisdom. After spending a couple of hours at the airport, I boarded the morning flight to Mumbai and rented a cab which cleverly manoeuvered its way through the clogged streets of the city.

I remembered all my incredible teachers of the past month as the cab got stuck, yet again, in bumper-to-bumper traffic. Duan Aimond, Feda Wahidi, Faline Cheong, Adaline Jones, Richard Omondi, Mandisa Kruger, Mark Adams, Brandon Smith, Captain Shyam Singh and Swami Sidheshwara were all remarkable people with invaluable insights into the world of finance and life. My interactions with them had made me more aware. How could I have hoped to make better choices in life, when I was not even aware I was indulging in self-defeating behaviors.

When I reached home, it was noon. But for me, it was like the dawn of a new beginning. My wife, son and daughter were overjoyed to see me after one whole month. But in the midst of all this euphoria, I felt an inexplicable grief, as though I had lost something. As I struggled to put my finger on the source of this overwhelming sense of sorrow, I remembered the letter that Swamiji had handed over to me.

I made a dash for my haversack, pulled out the envelope and tore it open.

The Final Letter

Dear Friend,

I have always believed in the power of a financial education. I have always believed that it is possible for each and every human being, irrespective of his current financial position, to attain complete financial freedom. I am pained to see how people deal with money. I feel distressed over the daily struggles of the poor to make ends meet. I feel the strain middle-class people suffer as they work even harder, struggle even more, deny themselves, paying huge amounts in taxes and interest, only to see their money being eaten up by inflation and finally, ending up in greater debt. I feel equally pained when I see the rich become richer at the expense of the poor and the middle-class. I believe that every individual has the right to fullfill his dreams, the right to an education, the right to proper medical care, the right to a good, peaceful retirement and the right to leave wealth to future generations and charity.

People see lack of money as a problem and believe that having lots of money is the way to overcome it. However, money is not the problem. The problem is lack of knowledge about money. As you have learned on your recent journey, it is the way you deal with money at the time of earning, protecting, budgeting, saving, spending, leveraging, investing and insuring that determines whether money becomes a solution or a problem for you. There is no point in envying the rich. They have learned the rules of money and applied them to their benefit. You can do the same.

These insights into financial wisdom are equally useful to students, because the problem with today's youth is that they earn a lot, spend more than they earn, buy liabilities with negative leverage, believing them to be assets, get in a debt trap and then become slaves to money for life. I feel very pained to see this and that is why I sent you on this journey.

Money is the only thing that is available in abundance in the world today. It is available at the free will of governments, limited only by how fast their printing machines can work. If you ask any government to give you unlimited amounts of gold, silver, copper, steel, oil, sugar, wheat or other real commodities, it will not be able to do so, because Mother Earth only offers these in limited quantities. But tell any government to give you paper money and it can give you an unlimited supply of it. All it has to do is print it. And if the government can print money, so can you, and that too, legally! That is what will take you from financial slavery to financial freedom. These are the thoughts which inspired me to make it my personal mission to educate people on money and its peculiarities.

You now know all about earning from the right source, protecting money, budgeting, investing, leverage, real estate, speculative items, spending, financial insurance, asset allocation, common financial mistakes, as well as the rules of money. You are now aware of the different forms of earning, how to earn from the right source, how to convert earned income into passive and portfolio income, generating life long cash flow for you with minimum or no taxation, the importance of paying yourself first via the creation of your budget surplus, protecting yourself from financial predators, the difference between saving and investing, safeguarding the value of your money against the monster of inflation, spending to get rich, the true place of speculative assets and the invincibility of financial insurance.

You are now privy to the following eternal truths:

- a job is not an asset. You can neither own a job, nor pass it on to your children
- a home is not an asset as it takes money out of your pocket
- money is not an asset. It is a debt and is rapidly being devalued with more national debt.
- a retirement plan is not an asset but an unfunded liability
- workers' savings are a source of cash for the true capitalists

You know all about issues, such as:

- the best sources and methods of earning income
- the best ways to invest
- how asset allocation is the secret to creating enduring wealth
- how to pay yourself first via a budget surplus

- how to make money from thin air
- liabilities disguised as assets
- how investment assets help set one financially free
- how to unleash the power of good debt to multiply one's wealth
- how to protect one's money from financial predators

At the same time, it's a heartbreaking reality that even today:

- children go to school, but learn nothing about money
- the youth come out of school looking for a job, anxious to get married, buy a home and raise a family
- the largest business in town, that of the government, is run by politicians and public servants, who know little about money, finance or investments
- the government relentlessly prints money, robbing you of your own money via inflation
- government taxes you indiscriminately, transferring money from consumers to capitalists
- those with jobs are only too happy to have taxes taken away from their salary before they get paid
- employees are only too happy to have their money deducted from their salary, thinking they are investing for their retirement while, in fact, they are funding the unfunded liability of the government
- people work for money rather than letting their money work for them

This is what happens when people don't know the difference between assets and liabilities. They spend their lives accumulating liabilities, believing them to be assets. They go to school to find a job without knowing that a job is not an asset. *They work for money, little realizing that money is no longer money.* They buy a house, completely oblivious to the truth that a house is not an asset. They save in government retirement plans without any knowledge that those funds are pooled cash for unfunded government liabilities. When they lose their jobs to younger, more efficient people, they go back to school to earn higher degrees, falling into the same cycle without any real chance of winning. Remember, the poor work to make it from day to day and the middle-class, to buy liabilities mistakenly believing they are assets, but the rich make their own and other people's money work for them.

My friend, before this new age of information and technology ends the financial future of our youth, I want you to change the education system, change the way people think and deal with money. Rather than leaving school to look for jobs, students should leave school looking for opportunities to create high-paying jobs. Rather than leaving school wanting to be paid more for less work, students should leave school seeking opportunities to produce more to earn more. Rather than leaving school believing the rich are greedy, students should leave school wanting to be the rich who are generous. Rather than leaving school to look for job security and becoming slaves to money, students should leave school to attain financial freedom.

I want you to set up a parallel education system where teachers will impart financial knowledge. Instead of teaching youngsters to be workers, teach them to be entrepreneurs; instead of teaching them to avoid risks, teach them to take calculated risks; instead of teaching them to run away from difficulties, teach them to face their difficulties; instead of teaching them to be losers, teach them to be winners; instead of teaching them to be slaves of money, teach them to be masters of money; instead of cursing them with slavery, bless them with financial freedom; instead of teaching them to use their financial wisdom to cheat and deceive the uneducated, encourage them to use it to teach, enlighten and set people free; instead of teaching them to use their financial wisdom to make only themselves richer, goad them to use it to enrich the lives of others. That is the only way you can pay back my debt – the debt of making you financially wise.

Today, millions of people around the world are losing their jobs to innovation, their homes to foreclosures, their retirement savings to fund government liabilities, their income to indiscriminate taxes, their purchasing power to inflation, their money to debt, their investments to the greed of the capitalists and their souls to financial slavery. Use this crisis to motivate yourself to do something good. Be a part of the solution, not the problem. Don't forget that human beings are entering a new era of humanity, an era of unlimited abundance, and opportunity. Advances in technology have reduced costs, decreased financial risks, reduced prices, brought down wages, and opened up world markets. Technology has made it easier for entrepreneurs. The bad news is that technology makes life difficult for employees. *Those who follow socialist ideas will continue to live a life of scarcity with low wages, higher taxes, money lost to inflation and their wealth stolen by fees and expenses by the very people to whom they entrust their wealth.* On the other hand, financially savvy people will live a life of abundance, with governments offering them tax breaks and inflation working in their favor. They will have their own and other people's money working for them through assets, leverage multiplying their wealth and money running after them.

And, my friend, you would have to do all this alone, because I will not be there with you. By the time you receive this letter, I may have departed from this world. I have been diagnosed with terminal lung cancer and was given only 30 days to live when I met you. I was looking for someone to pass on the baton to, to rid this world of financial slavery, and God sent you to me. Your 30-day world tour was to train you to be ready for your new job.

Like cancer, legalized corruption eats away at the moral fiber of the world. Men and women of power, craving more power, sell their souls to glorify their egos, destroying lives and bleeding the very people they are supposed to serve. Like me, the world is also suffering from cancer. Nobody can save me, but you can surely save this world. The ball is now in your court. First change yourself and then change the world.

Blessings,
Vijay Desai

I was sobbing uncontrollably. My mind was blank, my body numb. Finally, I gathered some courage and switched on the TV. News of his death was on all the channels. It was true, my dear friend was no more!

I remembered he had once said, "the only reason for improvement should be genuine desire from within oneself. Don't change to show the world, but make the change because it means the world to you.

God didn't promise days without pain, laughter without sorrow, sun without rain, but He did promise strength for the day, comfort for the tears and light for the way."

Truly, Vijay was an exceptional individual who had always selflessly and unendingly signified true humanity. A good Samaritan statesmanship, with marked virtues of an individual who had throughout life nurtured adversity and converted it into opportunity. These exceptional qualities made him an inspiration for others. My friend had given purpose to my life and that was to help people live a life of financial freedom, which is their birthright.

I was determined to carry on my friend's mission, moving people from financial slavery to financial freedom and justify my new lease on life, Vijay's gift to me. My friend's life had ended, but he had given my life a new beginning.

Epilogue

I am now 85 years of age and my life is nearly done. But, as you know now, this is not the first time I am lying on a hospital bed. Forty years ago, I met my friend and mentor, Vijay Desai, while on such a bed. Not only did he save my life, he gave me a new way of living. As a direct result of that, the quality and experience of my life has been tremendous at every moment.

Generally speaking, there are three kinds of people – those who look at the obstacles and don't start the journey, those who start the journey, but stop when confronted with the obstacles and those who start the journey bravely facing and conquering each obstacle on their way to ultimate victory. Those souls attain true freedom. I hope my story will inspire you to attain true lasting freedom.

I wish you all the very best as you begin your journey toward financial independence after having read mine. And when you reach that goal, I only ask that you help others by passing on what you have learned.

Forty years ago, I was on the same hospital bed, and waiting beside me was my childhood friend, Vijay Desai. Today also, he is beside me, but this time his soul is awaiting the moment for us to be reunited once again. I can't wait any longer to be with him and finally experience serenity.

These are the final moments for me on this planet. It seems that I can hear the whole world. The distant screaming of my fans and well-wishers, the sobbing of my family members, the wishes of the old, the love of the young, a rush of wind, the waves, the music, a loud ugly noise that I realize is the sound of my own breathing. I am going. My eyes are closing. I can see some blurred view across the horizon of my friend waiting with both his arms open for me. I need to go. But don't you forget my story. Don't forget my journey. Don't forget my incredible teachers around the world. Don't forget the great wisdom of my friend, Vijay Desai. Don't forget that you are born free and can always live freely without being a slave to money or life. Don't forget to find your path toward financial nirvana. I found mine. My work is over. I have to go. My friend is waiting for me. My eyes are closing. My eyes have closed. I have gone, but my story will remain with you forever. As the proverb goes, 'give a man a fish, and you feed him for a day. Teach him to fish and you feed him for a lifetime.'

About the Author

MEHRAB IRANI is a qualified chartered accountant, company secretary and CFA (Level I) with rich experience in investment research, portfolio management and investment banking. He has diverse experience of both equity and fixed income markets, including research, dealing and portfolio management. He has been responsible for managing the portfolios of a third party (mutual fund) and also proprietary money (corporate). He has also experience in investing in different categories of mutual funds, including equity, fixed income, and cash management. He has worked in Deloitte in the audit department, and has also done research on the US and European financial services sector, including investment banks, money center banks, commercial banks, retail banks, AMCs and investment companies, brokerage houses, insurance companies, independent research service providers, thrifts, etc.

Mehrab is fired by an almost missionary zeal for spreading financial knowledge among the masses and is utterly convinced that it is possible for anyone to become financially free. He has written numerous articles for many newspapers, magazines, finance, and investment journals, and online websites. His ability to connect abstract concepts and real life situations, using his powerful imagination and plethora of skills reverberates through all his work. He also appears on various TV channels in India, like CNBC, ET Now, NDTV Profit, Bloomberg TV, etc. Being a sought-after speaker, Mehrab also gives guest lectures across various corporate events, management institutions and colleges. He is also a famous voice on FM channels like Radio Mirchi. Mehrab's Financial Freedom program features unique workshops with a holistic approach to not just money, finance and investments but also on the self-discovery of life through inspiration, motivation and intuition. This can be achieved by reclaiming our higher self that may have become a captive to financial slavery. Mehrab brings with him a financial wisdom that explains the intense equation and challenges between man and money in this day and age. Through his special workshops, Mehrab works toward breaking the myths and illusions about money that have surrounded people for decades. He also writes a well-read blog: www.intelligentmoney.blogspot.com. Anybody can visit him at www.mehrabirani.com.

Mehrab is currently the General Manager of Investments with Tata Investment Corporation in Mumbai, India.

Mehrab can be reached at –
mehrabirani10@gmail.com.
www.twitter.com/RealMehrabIrani
www.facebook.com/authormehrabirani
www.instagram.com/mehrabirani

For more information on the book, please visit
www.facebook.com/madmoneyjourney
www.madmoneyjourney.com

Financial Freedom Game

I have come up with a unique set of board games called the Financial Freedom Game. These are aimed at imparting knowledge based on the Ten Financial Commandments expressed in the story for players to achieve financial freedom. They have been adapted for players of basic, intermediate, and expert levels, as well as one for children.

The complexity of the games vary from simply scrolling over the board to see how right decisions lead to financial freedom to how wrong decisions will put you to test in difficult situations. At every point, the players will have to make decisions like whether to invest more money on his higher studies or business; to budget extra money for the future or buy a car; to use limited available funds for important house repairs or a costly foreign vacation; to take a working capital loan to expand his business or a mortgage lan to buy a bigger house; to invest in shares or bonds or gold; to take positive leverage and expand business or just be content to stay small; whether to opt for financial insurance; how to create positive cash flow via leverage; how to do proper asset allocation and much more.

Play the most financially savvy game to achieve financial independence.

For further details contact me at: mehrabirani10@gmail.com

Visit my website: www.mehrabirani.com

Read my Blog: www.intelligentmoney.blogspot.com

Follow me on: www.twitter.com/RealMehrabIrani

My Facebook page is: www.facebook.com/authormehrabirani

Financial Freedom Course /
Corporate Speech

I believe every one of us desires and has a right to achieve financial independence. The loopholes in the education system are largely to be blamed for the ignorance and ineptness in dealing the single-most important element we deal with throughout our lives – money. We study mathematics, but never really learn the value of the numbers we employ. It is no wonder then that we end up as slaves to money than as the masters of it. As a result, millions in the world are suffering and fighting, because of the lack of it, despite it being available in abundance. The money is distributed unfairly: 10% of the population controls 90% of the wealth, whereas the 90% of people fight for the remaining 10% of wealth. In common economic jargon, this is defined as the 'unequal distribution of wealth'.

Given the times, young people enter a vicious cycle of working hard for money; paying more in taxes; letting their finances get swallowed up by the monster called inflation; being unable to protect their money; paying everyone but themselves; depending on others for their livelihood; and finally, on the government for their retirement.

My wish is for everyone to make their way out of financial slavery into financial nirvana.

In the past 15 years of money management, I have seen even educated, well-earning professionals like doctors and engineers struggle with their finances. This unfortunately includes women, irrespective of being home-makers or bread-winners, who leave money matters entirely to their spouses or families. We must do our utmost to change this mindset, so that future generations, no matter what their occupation, know how to cleverly deal with money.

If you view money as either a problem or a solution, then I am afraid that you are already a prisoner of money, because it is neither. What is really required is for us to understand money, its unique peculiarities and its functioning. Therefore, I have designed a course /workshop to cater to this growing need for financial freedom, without the need of expert knowledge on equities, bonds, commodities, real estate, currencies, etc., and slaving away to earn money.

If you are interested in getting acquainted with:

- The best source of earning income
- How to protect if from financial predators
- How to pay yourself first via budget surplus
- Acknowledging that saving is not investing and learning to save pending asset allocation
- Learning how to spend to earn and save at the time of spending
- Recognizing the difference between good and bad debt and how to unleash the power of positive leverage
- Knowing how to invest for proper asset allocation
- Recognizing the importance of financial insurance

Then enroll for this course to put an end to all your money worries.

Mehrab's Financial Freedom program is highly sought-after among esteemed and illustrious entrepreneurs as well as erudite members of the corporate world in India. The program is recommended for every organization that is ambitious and driven to make the most of the financial environment now and in the future. If you wish to explore the wonders of financial freedom and a stress-free life, invite Mehrab to your workshops or events for your employees, clients, associates and many more. His profound knowledge of financial wisdom may just be one of the most fruitful mantras for accomplishments across all corporate sectors..

If you simply want a friend or guide to fill you in on these issues, then contact me at the below mentioned email address.

I wish you all the very best as you embark on this new journey of money toward achieving financial independence.

For further details contact me at: mehrabirani10@gmail.com

Visit my website: www.mehrabirani.com

Read my Blog: www.intelligentmoney.blogspot.com

Follow me on: www.twitter.com/RealMehrabIrani

My Facebook page is: www.facebook.com/authormehrabirani

You may get in touch at: www.instagram.com/mehrabirani